# Practical Experiences with **Modelling** and **Forecasting Time Series**

D1350946

# Practical Experiences with Modelling and Forecasting Time Series

Gwilym.M.Jenkins

## Time Series Library

A GJP Publication

First published 1979
ISBN 0 9506 423 0 4.

Gwilym Jenkins & Partners (Overseas) Ltd.
39/41 Broad Street
St. Helier
Jersey, Channel Islands.


Printed and bound in the U.K. by Titus Wilson Ltd. Kendal.

# Contents

# Foreword to the Series

Time series analysis and forecasting is becoming one of the most important areas of development in statistical science. This series of books on time series analysis is a response to the growing importance of, and interest in, this rapidly evolving subject.

Time series analysis is being used in many branches of science and engineering and especially in the social and management sciences. The consulting statistician's work in this, and in other areas, begins when he has a client with a problem. Examination of the problem will reveal that the client is interested in certain objectives. In turn these objectives will lead to the formulation of certain hypotheses and to the need to collect data to examine the adequacy or inadequacy of these hypotheses. Advice will be needed first on what type of data is required and in what form it should be collected. Then models will need to be built using the data, in turn requiring a model building methodology flexible enough to be adapted to the particular problem in hand so that the hypotheses which do not explain the data can be quickly rejected and replaced by ones which do. Then the models must be related to the client's objectives, for example they may be used to generate information for taking decisions. Questions then arise as to how best to present and use this information.

Much of what is nowadays called 'mathematical statistics' has little to do with the process briefly described in the previous paragraph. In contrast, the genius of the late Sir Ronald Fisher was that he saw himself not only as a statistician but first and foremost as a scientist. Thus, we find major technical statistical advances 'tucked away' in papers primarily concerned with some important scientific problem. Fisher's concept of how to act as a consultant remains a model for today's generation of statisticians - and his work a perfect illustration of the fact that significant advances will be made when there is a *healthy interaction* between 'theory' and 'practice'.

This series of books on time series analysis is dedicated to the memory of Ronald Fisher and his work. It is directed at those scientists who have problems requiring the analysis of time series and at those statisticians who have to offer them advice. In particular, it is intended to publish books and other material describing statistical methodology useful for the solution of practical time series problems - and to illustrate this methodology with practical exam—ples. It is also intended to publish complete case studies describing the whole process from formulation of the original problem to the presentation and use of the final results.

G.M. Jenkins,
Lancaster.
March 1978.

# Preface

Data in the form of time series arise in many branches of the physical sciences, engineering, the biological sciences and the social sciences. The increasing interest in time series analysis in recent years arises partly because of its widespread applicability. For example, concepts useful for modelling competition between two or more animal populations are equally applicable to competition between two commercial products serving a common market. This *isomorphism* between models is, of course, a reflection of the similarities in structure between the corresponding systems. What we are concerned with, therefore, is a common mathematical language (usually referred to as 'models'), for describing *dynamic systems* and a set of concepts for *building* these models when both the inputs and outputs to the system are subject to statistical fluctuations or noise.

There are many reasons for wanting to build a model of a dynamic system. The first objective is *understanding* - what mechanisms are at work in influencing the outputs of the system? A second objective is *forecasting* - what is likely to happen to future values of the outputs if present management policies are maintained? Thirdly, it is important to generate *insight* into the behaviour of the system and, in particular, into the ways in which its performance might be improved in future - how does the system behave when it is *simulated,* making various assumptions about the future behaviour of the inputs? Finally, the ultimate objective in the study of many systems is some form of *optimisation* - a frequently misused term but intended to convey that steps are taken now so that, hopefully, future performance is better than it was in the past, or no worse than it was, in the light of changing environmental conditions.

In this book, we shall be concerned mainly with the first two of these objectives, namely understanding and forecasting. However it is emphasised throughout that forecasting is not an end in itself but a means to providing information for action, leading to improvement. As such, the book will be of interest not only to statisticians, management scientists, economists, scientists and engineers, involved in the forecasting process in a technical capacity, but also to their managers - those who have to use and act upon the forecasts provided by their technical advisors.

The book is based on two lectures given during the Institute of Statisticians Conference on Forecasting at King's College, Cambridge in July, 1976. It is published simultaneously as part of the proceedings of that Conference by the North - Holland Publishing Company. The object in part is to present, using a series of practical examples, an account of the models and model building methodology described in the book *Time Series Analysis, Forecasting and Control* by Professor George Box and the writer, published in 1970. A second objective is to present examples of the extensions to the methodology since that book was published. Foremost amongst these extensions are the modelling and forecasting of systems with *multiple outputs* and *intervention analysis* (the use of dummy variables to describe external events such as a strike or a change in a law).

To make the book more understandable to non - technical readers, where possible technical detail has been reduced to a minimum in the main body of the text. However, it is impossible to avoid using technical terms and to help some readers, a glossary of such terms is included at the end of the book. In explaining the technical details associated with some of the applications, it is assumed that the reader is familiar to a certain extent with the approaches to building univariate and transfer function models given in Box and Jenkins (1970). Accounts of the extensions of the methodology to deal with multivariate models and intervention analysis are given in the Appendices at the end of the book. However, these accounts are necessarily brief since the main objective here is to describe practical applications and not details of the methodology.

I am grateful to the many people who have collaborated with me in the consultancy work which lies behind the practical illustrations described here. These collaborators include Dr. Gordon McLeod who has made helpful comments on the final draft of the manuscript. I also thank The Fern Art Company, Kendal for producing diagrams of such high quality and Mrs. Elaine Morris and Miss Pennie Hardman for their diligence in typing an excellent manuscript.

G.M. Jenkins,
Lancaster.
February, 1978.

# Introduction

---
---

The world scene is characterised by increasing *uncertainty* about the future. There is some evidence to suggest that our social and economic systems are becoming more *unstable* and that, for example, the rapid rises in raw material prices, increasing pollution and exponential population growth are symptoms of that instability. In parallel with this increasing uncertainty, the consequences of bad decisions are becoming more costly in human, environmental and financial terms. As a result of these tendencies, and of growing social pressures for better planning, the importance of forecasting as a management activity is likely to increase.

As a profession, we as statisticians have a great deal to contribute to the activities of forecasting and planning. However, it is a pity that, unlike some of the pioneers of the profession, we have tended to concentrate in recent years on 'second order' mathematical issues remote from the solution of practical problems. It is a pity also that, when we do get involved in practical problems, we tend to see ourselves as specialists offering advice on the collection and analysis of data. But practical problems do not divide themselves readily into statistical and non-statistical components. To be effective in a practical context, we need to be concerned first with the solution of problems and second with the relevance of techniques, statistical or otherwise.

These considerations are especially true in the area of forecasting. Thus, in Part 1 we argue that forecasting needs to be viewed as part of the overall *management* process. Otherwise, it is likely to degenerate into a 'numbers game' played by 'backroom specialists', remote from the areas where decisions are taken. Part 2 outlines *five classes of model* which can be used to describe a spectrum of practical forecasting situations, ranging from the simple to the more complex. Part 3 contains *applications* of each of the five classes of model described in Part 2. Throughout Parts 2 and 3 emphasis will be placed on practical issues, associated with how the models helped to solve a particular problem, as well as on technical statistical issues. A more detailed description of the models, together with some guidelines on how to build them, is given in a series of Appendices. Part 4 contains a brief comparison of the approach outlined in Parts 1—3 with conventional *econometric approaches.*

# Part 1 Forecasting and Management

Part 1 emphasises the role which a forecasting activity in an organisation needs to play in order to contribute to planning and decision taking. It ends with some practical guidelines for tackling any forecasting problem.

## 1.1. An example of the consequences of poor forecasting

Figure 1a shows a weekly index, based on the spot price for chartering oil tankers, for the four year period 1968–71. In the spring of 1970 the index began to rise and prompted a few oil companies to conclude that prices would continue to increase for the forseeable future. This resulted in a switching from 'spot chartering' to 'futures chartering' in which longer term contracts were signed, based on a fixed price. In turn this additional demand created a world shortfall in tanker capacity, forcing up the price even higher. Encouraged by the fulfilment of their earlier prophesies, a few companies forecasted further price increases and took up further long term contracts, causing yet further capacity shortages, price increases and distortion of the market mechanism. After the effects of these and other disturbances (which caused the index to increase by more than twice its value over a period of nine months) had subsided, the index returned by mid-1971 to values similar to those which obtained in the early part of 1970. In the meantime considerable sums of money were lost as a result of contracts fixed at inflated prices. Similar large scale mistakes can be instanced in the area of commodity purchasing.

Figure 1b shows the series consisting of the first differences $z_t - z_{t-1}$ between the price index in consecutive weeks. To the eye, the series looks random and this is confirmed by more detailed statistical analysis. Thus, the apparent 'trend' in the index $z_t$ can be described adequately by the 'random walk' model

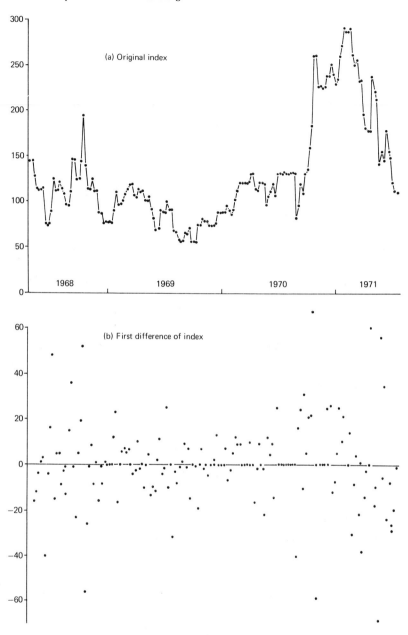

Fig 1. 'Spot' price index for tanker chartering and its first difference.

$$z_t - z_{t-1} = a_t \tag{A}$$

where $a_t$ is a series of 'random shocks' (in fact, a slightly better representation is obtained by the 'random walk' model for the logarithms of the series, i.e. $\ln z_t - \ln z_{t-1} = a_t$).

This example illustrates that the extrapolation of past trends based on inspection of the data can be highly misleading. Such 'trends' can be described more realistically by means of mechanisms such as (A), based on random shocks which continuously modify for example the 'level' of the series, as in (A). Conditional on the representational adequacy of the model (A), the 'best' forecast of next week's price (and of the price in all future weeks) is this week's price. Such a trivial forecast is unlikely to be very helpful in practice and so the next logical step would be an attempt to relate the price index to market variables such as the world supply and demand for tanker capacity and the basic variables which influence them. In this way, improvements in forecasting accuracy might be achieved as a result of a better understanding of market mechanisms.

## 1.2. *Forecasting as part of the overall management activity*

In addition to emphasizing the dangers associated with extrapolating 'trends' discerned by eye in the past history of a series, the example of Section 1.1 also illustrates the disastrous effects which bad forecasting can sometimes have on decision taking and management. 'Management' is central to the needs of mankind. It is concerned with the deployment of scarce *resources* to achieve *objectives* – the means by which ends are achieved in all social organisations. Forecasting is likely to be more effective if regarded as a *means* of achieving an organisation's objectives rather than as an end in itself. As illustrated in Figure 2, forecasts need to be tailored so that they serve an organisation's decision-taking and action systems. Failure to integrate forecasting with decision-taking may render useless what may be good forecasts and cause frustration to an organisation's forecasting advisers whose advice may be ignored by management.

Much confusion can follow from a failure to distinguish between forecasting, planning and control. Thus:

- a *forecast* can tell a manager what he can achieve if policy remains unchanged;
- a *plan* enables a manager to take action so as to *change the forecasts*. For example, the sales of a product may be stimulated by price changes, promotional activity and advertising (this has implications for the use of past sales

data for forecasting future sales since such forecasts may be misleading if the effects of price changes and advertising are not allowed for in the historical data);

— *control* involves monitoring when the forecast errors are larger than expected on a statistical basis, leading to corrective action if the forecast errors are abnormally high.

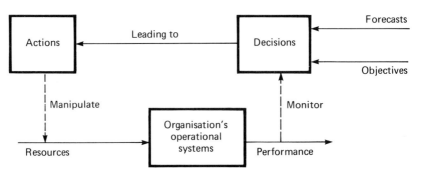

Fig 2. Forecasting as part of overall management activity.

The distinction between forecasting and planning made here is not an academic one. Frequently one finds that a *budget* is a forecast of past performance. Indeed, some organisations base their *corporate plans* on an extrapolation of past trends, producing extensions of the one year ahead budget and not plans designed to *change the forecasts*.

Figure 3 amplifies the relationship between forecasting and decision-taking shown in Figure 2. A distinction is made in the figure between *policy variables*, such as price and quality changes, which are under the control of management, and *external variables*, such as the activities of government and competitors, which also influence the variables being forecast but which are not under the control of management. In a real-life forecasting situation, based on forecasts of the external variables, forecasts of the variables of interest will be generated under the assumption that no changes in the policy variables are made. Then, if these forecasts are not satisfactory, policy variable changes will be made in order to make the forecasts more acceptable. Thus the forecast generating system needs to be seen as part of a *closed-loop* management system in which the 'forecasts' may be changed and become *out-of-date* as soon as they become available.

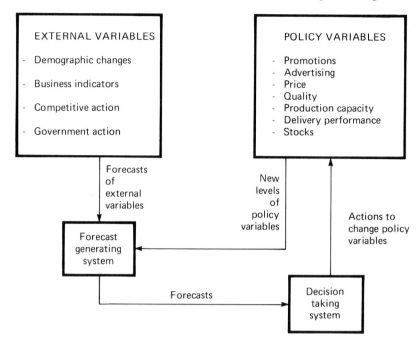

Fig 3. Role of forecast generating system in decision taking.

## 1.3. Some guidelines for tackling a forecasting problem

Table 1 shows a check-list of considerations that the writer has found useful in tackling problems associated with business forecasting. It is not suggested that it is exhaustive nor that all considerations in the list will be relevant to every situation.

Item 1 of the checklist involves an analysis of the decision-taking system to be served by the forecasts. By this is meant that the *decisions* and *actions* which need to be taken in a particular management system are set down. Not infrequently such an investigation may show up inconsistencies in the decision-taking process itself; for example, decisions for which responsibilities are not clearly defined or decisions for which the relevant information is not available, or is not made available in the right form to those who need it.

Item 2 involves setting down *what* forecasts are needed for decision-taking and *how* they are to be used. The forecasts need to be defined in terms of:
— the *variables* to be forecast (e.g. sales volume, market share, price);
— the *planning horizon* over which forecasts are needed (e.g. 1 month, 18 months, 5 years);

— the *frequency* with which forecasts are needed (e.g. weekly, monthly);
— the *accuracy* required, bearing in mind that there can sometimes be a trade-off between accuracy and other management action (e.g. stock control policy);
— the level of *aggregation* (e.g. individual product, group of products, major areas of business) and, very importantly, how to ensure *consistency* between forecasts at different levels.

Table 1
Some guidelines for the development of a forecasting system

1. Analyse *decision taking system* served by forecasts
2. Define *forecasts* needed to serve decision taking system
3. Develop *conceptual model* describing mechanisms influencing forecasts
4. Define *data* available and not-available
5. Develop *method* for generating forecasts
6. Conduct *experiments* to assess accuracy of forecasts
7. Determine how *judgements* are to be incorporated into forecasts
8. Implement *forecasting system*
9. Appraise retrospectively its *effectiveness*

Item 3 involves developing a *conceptual model* of the system which influences the variable, or variables, to be forecast. By this is meant setting down what prior knowledge, 'theory' and judgement has to tell us about the *mechanisms* (in qualitative terms) that influence the variables to be forecast. It requires discussion with those who possess expert knowledge so that their qualitative 'feel' for the situation can be set down and shared by all concerned. It may not always be possible to obtain a 'consensus' view of the mechanisms at work. However, even in these cases it is usually better to have an explicit 'model' available for discussion rather than that people should carry around loose and unformulated ideas in their heads. An example of a conceptual model for forecasting telephone demand is given in Figure 4. Such a conceptual model should attempt to describe the variables which affect the particular system being studied and the variables which influence that system — and which form part of the *environment* of the system.

Item 4 involves using the conceptual model to determine what data is available on the variables to be forecast and on the variables which influence the variables to be forecast. The identification of gaps in data availability and reliability may have a considerable bearing on the approach to be adopted in building a forecasting model in item 5.

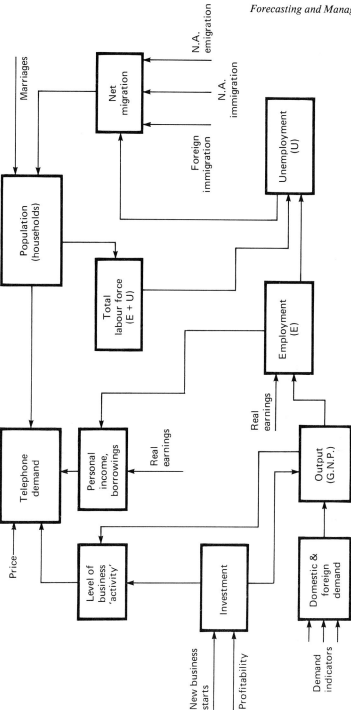

Fig. 4. Conceptual model for residential and business telephone demand in a North American (N.A.) State.

Item 5 itself is based on the assumption that some form of *quantitative model* will be built to generate the forecasts. The nature and sophistication of this model will depend on many factors, including the following:
— the forecast *accuracy* demanded by the decision-taking system;
— the *availability* of data and its *reliability*;
— the extent to which it is possible to find *policy* and *environmental* variables to improve the accuracy of the forecasts and to enable policy simulations to be attempted;
— the *cost* of developing the model, storing data and operating the system on a routine basis;
— the computational and model building *skills* available to the organisation.

If item 5 has been carried out in a meaningful way, the quantitative model should not only provide a means of generating forecasts but also of characterising their accuracy at different lead times, e.g. a standard deviation of 5% of the level at one step ahead, 7% two steps ahead, etc. Provided that there is enough data available, it is worthwhile going further (item 6) and comparing forecasts at various lead times generated by the model with actual data not used in the model building process. In this way, empirical measures of forecasting accuracy can be built up and compared with the theoretical predictions of accuracy obtained from the model. In this way confidence can be built up in the model and abnormal performance highlighted.

The use of a model presupposes that the statistical behaviour of the future will be similar to the statistical behaviour of the past. However, if it is believed that some future events are likely to be untypical of past behaviour, then some scope is needed for making adjustments to the forecasts obtained from the model. This 'tuning' (item 7) is a judgemental matter and depends on 'intelligence' not available to the model (for example a major new customer is expected in the next year or a competitor is to bring new capacity on-stream). The combination of forecasts obtained from past data and a model (*intrinsic* forecasts) with forecasts obtained by exercising judgement (*extrinsic* forecasts) is an important feature of any practical forecasting situation.

One of the biggest criticisms that can be made of the use of scientific methods in management is the inadequate attention paid to *implementation* — to 'making things happen' (item 8). For example, the writer has occasionally met organisational situations where forecasts based on quantitative models have consistently out-performed judgemental forecasts produced by management, but yet have been ignored. These situations occur because the role which the forecasting model should play in the management system has not been

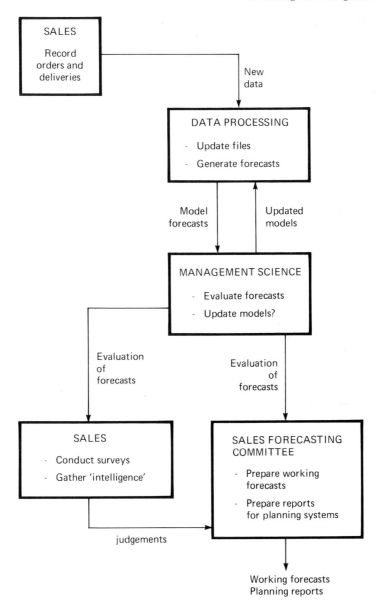

Fig 5. Activities, information flows and responsibilities in forecast generating system for a manufacturing company.

properly thought out. The activity involved under item 8 is an attempt to minimise the possibility of this happening. It involves an agreed statement with management as to the role of the forecast generating system in terms of:

— *what* needs to be done;
— *who* is responsible for doing it.

In particular, the statement should aim to clarify how:

— data is to be collected on an on-going basis and its accuracy verified;
— forecasts are to be generated using the data base, model and, if necessary, a computer;
— forecasts are to be modified by judgemental factors;
— forecasts are to be fed to the decision-taking system;
— forecast accuracy is to be evaluated;
— responsibilities are to be allocated for different aspects of the activity.

Figure 5 shows at a broad level of detail how a forecasting system was implemented in one particular manufacturing organisation.

Finally, when forecasts are being used on a routine basis, it is important to *monitor* and *appraise* the performance of the forecasting system (item 9). It involves:

— designing statistical tests to check that the one step ahead forecast errors are *random* with mean zero and a specified standard deviation as defined by the model;
— taking action if they are not random, e.g. by adjusting 'anomalous' data, updating the model, bringing in new variables, etc.

To summarise, too much emphasis on statistical and model building techniques at the expense of the broader issues discussed in this section may result in an ineffective forecasting system, even if the statistical analysis is well done.

# Part 2 Five classes of time series models

This part contains a non-technical description of five classes of models which have been developed to deal with a wide range of practical situations. In particular:

- Section 2.1 discusses the usefulness of *univariate models* for forecasting a time series from its own past history. Univariate models are described in detail in Box and Jenkins (1970) and are summarised in Appendix A.2.
- Section 2.2 discusses the role of *transfer function models* for relating an output time series, which is to be forecast, to a set of related input variables. These models enable a time series to be forecast not only from its own past history but also from the past history of other related variables. Transfer function models are described in detail in Box and Jenkins (1970) and in Appendix A.3 where they are extended to deal with relationships between seasonal time series.
- Section 2.3 describes a class of models, called *intervention models*, which can be used to represent unusual events such as a strike, a holiday or a change in definition of a variable. Intervention models are discussed in Tiao, Box and Hamming (1975) and in Appendix A.4.
- Section 2.4 describes the objectives of a class of models, called *multivariate stochastic models*, which can represent several output series with mutual interactions or feedback. A description of these models is given in Appendix A.5.
- Section 2.5 contains a brief account of models, called *multivariate transfer function models*, which can be used to relate several mutually interacting output variables to several input variables. These models have features in common with what econometricians call *simultaneous equation models*. A brief account of multivariate transfer function models is given in Appendix A.6.

— Section 2.6 presents some guidelines for building models in general and emphasises the need to understand the objectives of those for whom the model is designed. More detailed guidelines for building the five classes of models introduced in Sections 2.1–2.5 are given in the Appendix.

### *2.1. Univariate stochastic (single output) models*

The simplest forecasting situation occurs when one is asked to forecast the future of a time series from a knowledge of its past history only. For example, the upper part of Figure 6 shows a quarterly series of telephone installations for which forecasts are needed on a rolling basis up to 2 years ahead. Such a 'simple minded' approach could not be expected to produce very accurate forecasts over the long term. However, the use of an appropriate *univariate stochastic model* (see Box and Jenkins, 1970 and Appendix A.2) to generate forecasts from the past history of a series is important for several reasons:

(1) in some situations, for example in planning the production of several hundreds of manufactured products, it may be the only feasible practical approach to adopt because of the sheer magnitude of the problem;

(2) in other situations, it may be impossible to find variables which are related to the variable being forecast, leaving the univariate model as the only means for forecasting;

(3) even in situations where related variables may be used to improve the accuracy of the forecasts, the development of a univariate model provides a 'yardstick' with which more sophisticated models can be compared;

(4) the presence of large residuals in a univariate model may correspond to abnormal events, such as a strike, or to faulty data. Thus univariate models provide a valuable tool for *screening data* during the early stages of an analysis and for taking appropriate action if the cause of such large residuals can be identified (See Section 2.3).

In general, however, one would not expect univariate models to perform satisfactorily for forecasting at longer lead times if other variables which are related to the variable being forecast fluctuate in ways which are not typical of their behaviour in the past.

In addition to their use for forecasting, univariate models can lead to an *increased understanding* of the basic mechanisms generating a time series. For example, the presence of autoregressive operators with complex roots is indicative of some underlying cycle, such as a business cycle.

Practical examples of univariate models will be given in Section 3.1.

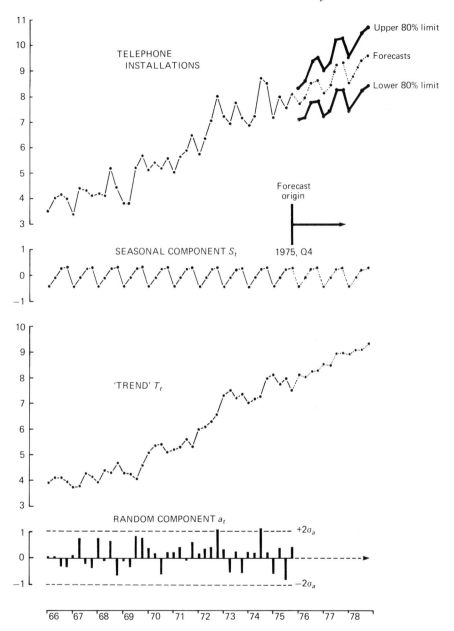

Fig 6. Decomposition of telephone installation series and forecasts from origin 1975, Quarter 4: quarterly data for the period 1966(1)−1975(4).

## 2.2.  *Transfer function (single output–multiple input) models*

If the data is available, and the effort is justified, it may be possible to improve upon the accuracy of the forecasts of an *output* (dependent) variable by introducing into the model other *input* (independent) variables which influence the output variable. This problem is not as easy as it sounds. As shown by M. S. Bartlett (1935), the correlations between two completely unrelated time series which are themselves internally correlated (autocorrelated) can sometimes be very large due to chance alone. Similarly, a regression coefficient, computed in the ordinary way, between two completely unrelated time series, but which are highly autocorrelated, may often be quite large.

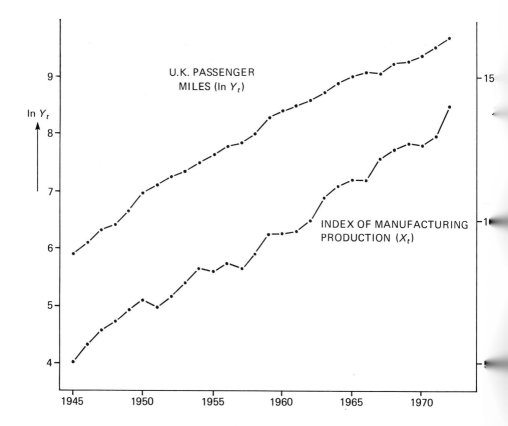

Fig 7. Two time series consisting of the logarithms of the number of passenger miles carried by all U.K. airways (ln $Y_t$) and the corresponding U.K. index of manufacturing production ($X_t$): annual data for the period 1945–72.

Figure 7 shows an 'output' series $\ln Y_t$ consisting of the natural logarithms of the total passenger miles travelled annually by passengers on all U.K. airlines and an 'input' series $X_t$ consisting of an annual index of manufacturing production. Figure 8 shows a scatter diagram of $\ln Y_t$ against $X_t$, from which it might be concluded that there is a strong relationship between the two variables. Not surprisingly, the regression coefficient between $\ln Y_t$ and $X_t$ is large compared with its standard error, calculated in the usual way. However, the large correlation and regression coefficients occur because $\ln Y_t$ is highly correlated with $\ln Y_{t-1}$ and $X_t$ in turn is highly correlated with $X_{t-1}$ thus producing a spuriously high correlation between $\ln Y_t$ and $X_t$. However, if one calculates the (partial) correlation between $\ln Y_t$ and $X_t$, having allowed for the correlation between $\ln Y_t$ and $\ln Y_{t-1}$, and the correlation between $X_t$ and $X_{t-1}$, (Quenouille, 1952), there is no evidence of any relationship between $\ln Y_t$ and $X_t$. This device is related to the principle of *prewhitening* (see Box and Jenkins, 1970). Figure 9 shows the cross correlation function between the two series at different *lags* relative to each other, *before* and *after* prewhitening. The cross correlation function before prewhitening is entirely misleading. However, the prewhitened cross correlation function shows that there is no evidence of a relationship between the two series at any lag.

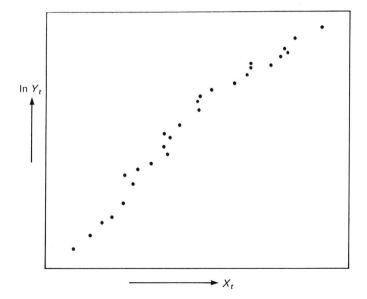

Fig 8. Scatter diagram of log passenger miles versus index of manufacturing production.

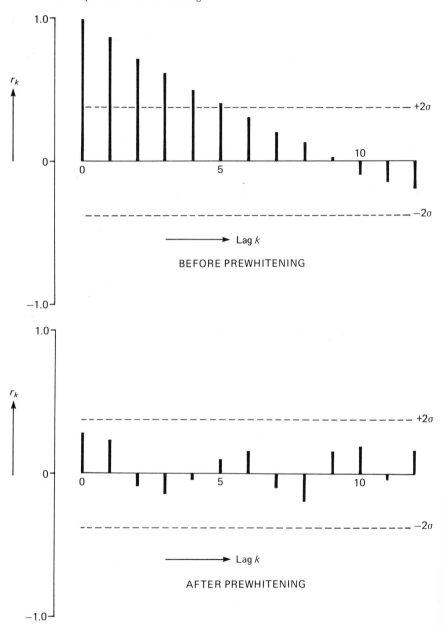

Fig 9. Cross correlation function between log passenger miles and index of manufacturing production before and after prewhitening, together with their two standard error ($\pm 2\sigma$) limits, under the assumption that the series are uncorrelated.

Econometric relationships in the form of regression relationships between time series are usually quoted with values of $R^2$ (the square of the multiple correlation coefficient) which measures in ordinary regression analysis the closeness of the fit between the output variable and the inputs. Values of $R^2$ as high as 0.95 or 0.99 are recorded quite frequently with econometric models, but these values are sometimes spurious (as is the value of $R^2$ between ln $Y_t$ and $X_t$ in Figure 8) for the reasons given above. Thus, in time series analysis, great care is needed in relating two or more time series. For the time series of Figure 7, it is not being suggested that increases in the index of manufacturing production are not associated with increases in airline passenger travel. Clearly, an increase in manufacturing production results in an increase in air travel by businessmen and an increase in holiday travel by individuals because of increasing prosperity. However, insofar as changes in $X_t$ influence, or are associated with, ln $Y_t$, those influences are already reflected in the past history of the ln $Y_t$ series – there is no *additional information* in the $X_t$ series. Thus, in building *transfer function models* (see Box and Jenkins (1970) and Appendix A.3) relating an output series $Y_t$ to an input series $X_t$, or more generally several input series $X_{1t}, X_{2t}, \ldots, X_{mt}$, the question being asked is, given that the effect of $X_t$ on $Y_t$ may already be contained in the past history of $Y_t$, is there any *additional* information contained in $X_t$?

Whereas univariate models can often result in an empirical understanding of the underlying mechanisms generating the series, transfer function models can be used not only for forecasting but also for gaining an increased *understanding* of the behaviour of some *system*, be it physical, biological or social. Therefore, such models should be based not only on an empirical approach to the analysis of the data, but also on an understanding of the underlying mechanisms in the appropriate system. Practical examples of transfer function models will be given in Section 3.2.

## 2.3. 'Intervention' models

In some situations it is known that certain exceptional external events have affected the variables being forecast. For example, Figure 10 shows a series consisting of the monthly sales of a consumer product which is subject to regular promotional activity. Such promotions involve some temporary inducement to purchase a product and are sometimes difficult to quantify. In Figure 10 those months during which promotional activity took place are characterised by a *dummy variable* in the form of an 'impulse' of unit height and those months for which there is no promotion are characterised by zeros. The sales series can then be related to the 'promotions series' by a transfer function model of the type described in Section 2.2. This transfer function model can be used to explore various hypotheses concerning the dynamic (or lagged) relationship between promotions and sales. Such dynamic models, involving the use of dummy variables as input variables, are called *intervention models* (see, for example, Tiao, Box and Hamming, 1975). Practical applications of intervention analysis during the past few years have included the following:

— the effect of different kinds of promotional activity on sales;
— the effect of strikes (represented by impulses) on the sales volume and prices of manufactured products and the prices of commodities;

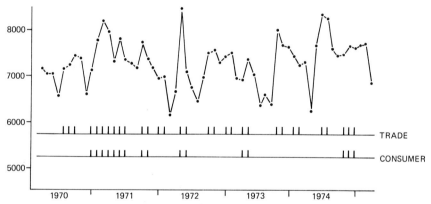

Fig 10. Sales of a consumer product subject to trade and consumer promotional activity: monthly data from April 1970 to April 1975.

— the effect of changes in policy or legislation (represented by a 'step function' consisting of 'zeros' before the policy change and 'ones' after the change) on business and economic time series;
— the effect of changes in definition (represented by a step function) on economic time series and relationships between such series.

As indicated in Section 2.1, the effect of an event, such as a strike, or a holiday, may be to produce one or more large residuals in the univariate model. Such large residuals may have a distorting influence on:

(i) the structure of the model tentatively entertained at the identification stage,

(ii) the values of the estimated parameters,

(iii) the magnitude of the residual variance.

Further details relating to intervention analysis are given in Appendix A.4 and some practical examples in Section 3.3.

## 2.4. *Multivariate stochastic (multiple output) models*

The transfer function models referred to in Section 2.2 assume that the input variables $(X_{it})$ affect the output variable $(Y_t)$ being forecast but that $Y_t$ in turn does not affect each $X_{it}$. The assumptions underlying such a *uni-directional* model may not always be justified in practice due to *feedback* between the output and the inputs. For example, Figure 11 shows the well known pair of

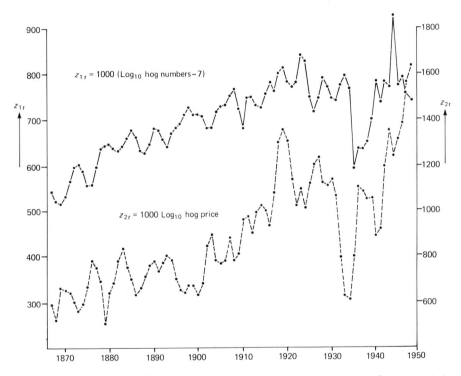

Fig 11. Logarithms of U.S. hog numbers and hog price: annual data for the period 1867–1948.

time series (see Quenouille, (1957)) consisting of the annual *number* of hogs sold in the United States and the corresponding *price* of hogs at January 1st of each year. Clearly, if the number of hogs increases this year, there is a tendency for the price of hogs next year to fall due to an excess of supply. Conversely, however, if the price of hogs falls this year, there will be a tendency for a fall in numbers next year as farmers cut back production due to a lack of incentive.

As a further example, Figure 12 shows two time series consisting of the sales volume per quarter of a certain group of consumer products and the corresponding advertising expenditure. It is seen that high advertising expenditure occurs at the same times that sales are high. This can partly be explained by the fact that high advertising expenditure increases sales. However, there is also evidence in this situation to suggest that advertising is increased as sales revenue is increased.

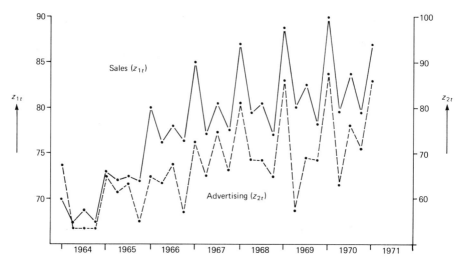

Fig 12. Sales volume and advertising expenditure for a group of consumer products: quarterly data for the period 1964(1)–1971(1).

Thus, advertising expenditure affects sales and simultaneously sales affect advertising expenditure.

In situations of the kind illustrated by the above two examples it is important not to treat one of the variables as the input and the other as the output in a transfer function model. This is because the transfer function so estimated will be a complex mixture of the 'forward transfer function' relating the input to the output and the 'backward transfer function' relating the output to the input. To deal effectively with such situations it is necessary to treat both variables (in general, the several variables involved) on an equal or reciprocal basis so that the two way feedback between each pair of variables can be disentangled. This requires the building of *multivariate stochastic models* (or multiple output models) to describe the *mutual dependence* between the variables. Such a model can then be used to simulate the behaviour of a multivariate system or to

generate simultaneous forecasts of the variables. Practical applications of multi-variate stochastic models during the past few years have included the following:
— the analysis of interactions between competitive products;
— the simultaneous forecasting of the number of telephones installed and the number of telephones disconnected in a particular geographical area;
— the simultaneous forecasting of stocks and different types of bonds in order to investigate alternative investment strategies for a pension fund;
— the interactions between imports, production and stocks of raw materials and associated manufactured products.
Further details relating to multivariate stochastic models are given in Appendix A.5 and a practical example in Section 3.4.

## 2.5. Multivariate transfer function (multiple output–multiple input) models

The multivariate stochastic models described in Section 2.4 can sometimes suffer from similar disadvantages to the univariate stochastic models referred to in Section 2.1, namely that they may perform unsatisfactorily if other variables, related to the variables being forecast on a simultaneous basis, behave in the future in ways which are not typical of their past behaviour. If these 'omitted variables' have two way feedback with the variables in the model, they will need to be introduced as further output variables. However, if it is known, or it is reasonable to assume, that their affect on the variables being forecast is uni-directional, then they may be introduced into the model as inputs. Thus, in general, the model will contain several outputs and several inputs. For example, Figure 13 shows two output variables, consisting of the monthly sales of two competitive products at simultaneous times and two input variables, consisting of their corresponding prices.

The multiple output–multiple input models referred to in this section are similar in concept to what would be referred to in econometrics as *simultaneous equation models*. However, as indicated in Appendix A.6, the models considered here have more general lag and error structures than those used in the past*. Examples of practical applications of multiple output–multiple input models during the past few years have included the following:
— the simultaneous control of the viscosity and specific gravity of a chemical product by means of two manipulated variables;

---

*In particular, they allow general ways for all input variables to influence all the output variables (cross-coupled dynamics) and all the errors to influence each other mutually (cross-coupled noise), as explained in Appendix A.6.

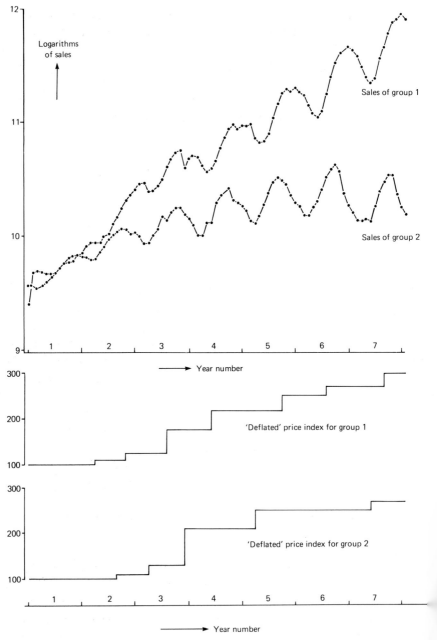

Fig 13. Sales of two groups of intermediate products, together with corresponding deflated price indices: monthly data for a period of 7 years.

— the effect of price changes and advertising on the sales of competitive products in order to simulate alternative pricing and advertising policies;
— the effect of interest rates and other economic variables on the flows of money into different categories of savings in order to investigate the effect of changes in relative interest rates.

Further details of multiple output—multiple input models are given in Appendix A.6 and a practical example in Section 3.5.

## 2.6. Building time-series models

The models, briefly summarised in the Appendix, are capable of representing a wide class of time series occurring in practice. In particular, they can be used to describe many types of:
— non-stationarity,
— seasonality,
— dynamic lag structures,
— mutual dependence or mutual feedback,
— cross-coupled dynamic lag structures,
— known external events by means of dummy variables in the form of impulses, step functions, ramps, etc.

The existence of such a wide class of representationally useful models is no guarantee that they can be successfully applied to a given practical situation. The preoccupation of some statisticians with mathematical problems of dubious relevance to real-world problems has been based on the mistaken notion that statistics is a branch of mathematics – in contrast to the more sensible notion that it is *part of the mainstream of the methodology of science*. The main activity of science is the development of 'models' to describe the real world and the design of experiments to test the representational adequacy of such models, leading to their *criticism* and further modification. The building of time series models needs to be approached in such a spirit – and with added caution since many time series arise in the social sciences where planned experimentation is possible only on a very limited scale and hence great care is needed with model criticism.

Table 2 contains some guidelines for building models in general. In the following discussion, emphasis will be placed on building forecasting models for planning and control.

Step 1 concentrates on understanding the problem to be solved and on the objectives of the model. Failure to understand the problem may mean that the model is irrelevant.

Step 2 is concerned with understanding the decision taking system surrounding the problem area and the role which the model will play in that system (Section 1.3 provides some guidelines).

Step 3 involves working out how the model is to be used on an on-going basis since this may have a bearing on what type of model is to be developed in the first place. Figure 5 is an example of how one set of forecasting models was implemented in a manufacturing company.

Step 4 is concerned with *structuring* the quantitative model: with understanding the system which influences the variable or variables being forecast.

Table 2
Some guidelines for building models for forecasting, planning and control

---

1.  Understand the *problem* and the *purpose* of building the model.
2.  Understand the *decision-taking system* which the model will serve.
3.  Work out early on how the model is to be *implemented*.
4.  *Structure* the quantitative model by building a conceptual model of the appropriate environmental system, displaying the mechanisms involved.
5.  Select the *data* carefully, understand its limitations and plot it in a variety of ways.
6.  Aim for *simple models*, involving few variables, first and then elaborate later, if necessary.
7.  Proceed *iteratively* via

    − Identification (Specification)
    − Estimation (Fitting)
    − Checking (Criticism)

8.  Aim for *parsimony* in parameterisation − avoid over parameterisation.
9.  Understand what the model has to say about the data.
10. Conduct *experiments* with the model (simulations) to understand its limitations.
11. *Present* the results from the model in simple terms to those who have to use it.

---

Rather than 'pluck variables out of the air' for inclusion in the model, the outcome of this important step is a conceptual model (such as Figure 4) which displays the *mechanisms* underlying the relationships in the model. This should lead to a better choice of variables for inclusion in the model and the identification of gaps in data availability.

Step 5 deals with selecting the data and understanding its limitations. In this connection, it is important to ensure that:

(a) the data is defined in a consistent way, for example by correcting for the number of delivery or working days in a month; otherwise it may be necessary to build parameters into the model which are compensating for the lack of consistency in the definition of the data*,

(b) gross recording errors are avoided by plotting the data and its successive differences,

(c) special events (such as strikes, holidays, production breaks) which might distort the data, are noted so that they can be allowed for in the model building process by means of intervention variables.

This step in the model building process is summarised by the statement that the statistician should 'fall in love with his data'.

Step 6 draws attention to the need to start model building by developing univariate models for the variables to be forecast and then introducing the explanatory variables one at a time. In this way, an orderly development can take place, checking that models are of minimum complexity and ensuring that variables are introduced only if they contribute. A useful dictum here is 'to learn to grovel before attempting to walk'.

Step 7 constitutes the main technical model building stages, (Box and Jenkins, 1970). *Identification* (or specification) of forecasting models involves the use of rough data analysis tools (range-mean plots, correlation and partial correlation functions) to arrive at *initial guesses* of the data transformations, degrees of differencing needed to induce stationarity and the degrees of the polynomials appearing in the various autoregressive and moving average operators appearing in the model (see the Appendices). *Estimation* (or fitting) involves using fully efficient (likelihood) methods for estimating the parameters, their standard errors and correlations, and the residual variances and covariances. Since no model can ever be 'correct', *checking* (or criticism) is an important step which involves looking for model *inadequacies* or for areas where *simplification* can take place. The most important model criticism criteria are:

— the residuals left unexplained by the model — are there any abnormally large residuals which can be linked to known external factors or other explanatory variables?

— the residual *correlations* and *partial correlations* — do they provide evidence that the model can be elaborated in a particular direction?

Whereas 'falling in love with the data' is a useful dictum in the early stages of

---

*For example, monthly data, uncorrected for the number of working or delivery days, can sometimes require a model containing a non-seasonal autoregressive operator $(1 - \phi_1 B - \phi_2 B^2)$ with complex roots and a period of approximately 3 months (the latter arises due to the presence of one 'short' month in approximately every three months). Correction by dividing by the number of working days will usually lead to the disappearance of the second-order autoregressive operator from the model.

model building, at the criticism stage the model builder should avoid, at all costs, 'falling in love with his model'!

Step 8 is linked with Step 7. When building models iteratively, it is important to achieve *parsimony* in parameterisation (another example of Occam's razor). Incorrect specification of the model structure can lead to the prodigal use of parameters, large standard errors and highly correlated estimates, as sometimes occur in econometiic models.

Step 9 is an attempt to understand what the model has to tell us about the data. Ultimately, any model must make sense and generate insight into the way that the data behave and into the mechanisms involved in the construction of the conceptual model (Step 4). In the case of time series models, insight can be gained by factorising the operators into real and complex factors. Thus, the sign of a negative root or the period of a complex root may tell us a great deal about the underlying mechanisms. In the case of transfer function models, considerable interest attaches to the *gains* associated with the independent variables. By a 'gain' is meant the ultimate change in an output variable as a result of a unit change in an input variable. When both output and input are measured on a logarithmic scale, a gain corresponds to what an economist would refer to as an *elasticity*.

Step 10 is a recognition of the fact that no model can be fully understood until *planned experiments* are performed with it. Where the model is to be used to select the 'best' values of the input variables (optimisation), the experiments will take the form of *simulations* of the possible outputs corresponding to different time profiles of the inputs. Where the model is to be used to generate forecasts, subsequently to be used as inputs to a planning or control system, it is important to obtain an understanding of the forecasting performance of the model. The model itself can be used to predict the standard deviations of the forecast errors at different lead times. Also, if possible, data withheld at the model building stage should be used to compare forecasts with actual values, leading to empirical standard deviations of the forecast errors at different lead times.

Step 11 considers how the results from the model can be presented in simple terms and is worthy of particular attention. Figure 6 illustrates how the forecasts from a univariate model for telephone installations were presented in a form which decomposed both data and forecasts into the components explained by the model.

The Appendices contain flow diagrams describing detailed approaches to model building for each of the model types introduced in previous sections.

Whereas these guidelines, and the more general guidelines of Table 2, can be helpful, providing stepping stones for the model builder to proceed in a systematic way, it must be remembered that model building is a highly creative process — as such, much depends on the skill of the model builder. However, it is believed that the approaches to model building presented here and in the Appendices, together with the associated computer programs, enable the analyst to experiment with his data and to exercise his creativity in a more successful manner than would have been possible otherwise.

# Part 3 Applications

This part contains applications of the five types of model introduced in Part 2 and described in greater detail in the Appendix. In particular:
— Section 3.1 describes the use of a set of univariate stochastic models to generate forecasts each month on a rolling basis to assist in operational planning in a medium sized company in the process industries.
— Section 3.2 describes three applications of transfer function models. In Section 3.2.1 an account is given of a study in which the market share of a group of consumer products is related to relative price and relative advertising, as an aid to decision-taking relating to the levels of price and advertising. Section 3.2.2 describes a model relating national electricity consumption to temperature, as an aid to the planning of electricity generating capacity. Section 3.2.3 describes models relating manufacturing employment to manufacturing output, forming part of a study to generate forecasts for decision takers concerned with employment policy.
— Section 3.3 describes two applications of intervention analysis. In Section 3.3.1, an account is given of an intervention model to allow for a change in credit policy in a study concerned with the forecasting of bad debt. Section 3.3.2 describes a set of intervention models designed to investigate the effect of various types of sales promotions on the sales of consumer products.
— Section 3.4 describes an application of multivariate stochastic models to the forecasting of sales of two competitive products in the European market.
— Finally, Section 3.5 describes an application of multivariate transfer function models (2 outputs — 4 inputs) to the investigation of relationships between sales and prices of two competitive products.
It is assumed in these accounts of practical applications that the reader has some familiarity with the model building approaches given in Box and Jenkins

(1970) for univariate and transfer function models. The Appendices summarise these model building approaches and give more detail in the case of intervention models, multivariate stochastic models and multivariate transfer function models since little has been published for these three classes of models up to the present. However, these accounts are necessarily brief in a publication of this kind where the main objective is to describe applications and not details of methodology.

## 3.1 An Application of Univariate Models to Operational Planning

The work was carried out for a company in the process industries in which there was little formal planning prior to this study. The remit for this project was to *design* and *implement* a planning system for taking operational decisions and to support this system with appropriate forecasting procedures.

The planning system had a horizon of 18 months and incorporated a linear programming model which was used to plan:
— production levels at each of 6 manufacturing sites,
— the utilisation of individual production units at each site,
— stocks of raw materials and intermediate products,
— deliveries between works and depots,
— hiring and purchasing of delivery vehicles.

The forecasts of total company sales were the most important. Because the company's share of the market was fairly stable, it turned out that total company sales could be forecast equally well by:

(a) projecting total company sales, or

(b) projecting total industry sales and then multiplying by the forecast of the (stable) market share.

These two forecasts are not always equally accurate and it may be necessary to try both ways in a given situation in order to determine which approach is best suited to the need at hand.

In addition to forecasts of total company sales, regional forecasts were needed to enable multi-site production schedules, raw material stocks and intermediate stock transfers to be planned. Figure 14 shows simple twelve-month moving averages of the sales of a group of products in three regions. Having removed most of the seasonality by this simple device, it is seen that the visual appearance of the series is markedly different from one region to the next, suggesting that different forecasting models might be needed in each region.

Univariate models were fitted to monthly sales data from each of five regions. The usual steps of identification, estimation and checking (see Table 2) were

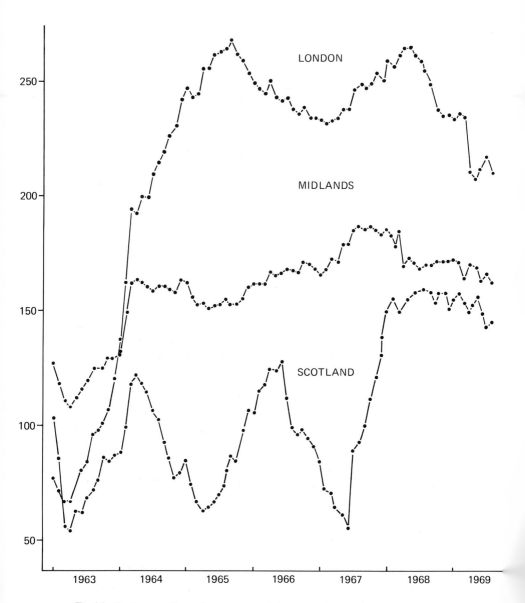

Fig 14. Twelve-month moving averages of the invoiced sales of a group of products in three different geographical regions.

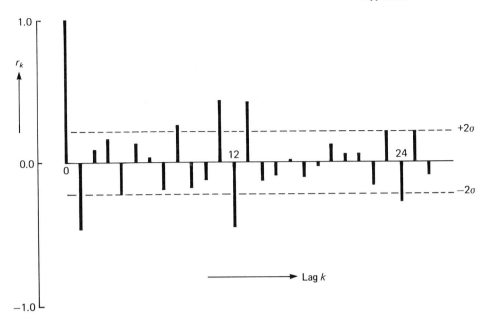

Fig 15. Typical autocorrelation function $r_k$ of $\nabla\nabla_{12}z_t$, where $z_t$ represents the monthly sales in one of the regions, based on 102 monthly observations. (The $\pm 2\sigma$ limits represent the two standard error limits under the assumption that the differenced series $\nabla\nabla_{12}z_t$ is random.)

applied to each series. The series contained significant trends, requiring non-seasonal differencing $\nabla$ to induce stationarity, and significant seasonal patterns, requiring further seasonal differencing $\nabla_{12}$ to induce stationarity in the seasonal behaviour. Figure 15 shows the autocorrelation function of $\nabla\nabla_{12}z_t$ for one of the regions, based on eight and a half years of monthly data. Since the autocorrelation function has values which are large compared with their standard errors at lags 1, 12, 24 and 'satellite' peaks at $12 \pm 1$, $24 \pm 1$, an initial model

$$\nabla\nabla_{12}z_t = (1 - \theta B)(1 - \Theta_1 B^{12} - \Theta_2 B^{24})a_t$$

is suggested. Table 3 shows the final models fitted to company sales and total industry sales for the whole of the U.K. and for the 3 regions shown in Figure 14.

The table shows that:

(1) the models for different regions are similar in structure despite the fact that the visual appearance of the data is different (See Figure 14 for 12-month

Table 3

Summary of univariate models fitted to sales data for (a) the whole industry, (b) the company, in different regions.

| Geographical region | Fitted models |
|---|---|
| Total U.K. (industry) | $\nabla\nabla_{12}z_t = (1-0.74B)(1-0.75B^{12} + 0.25B^{24})a_t$ |
| Total U.K. (company) | $\nabla\nabla_{12}z_t = (1-0.74B)(1-0.70B^{12} + 0.20B^{24})a_t$ |
| London region (industry) | $\nabla\nabla_{12}z_t = (1-0.74B)(1-0.62B^{12})a_t$ |
| London region (company) | $\nabla\nabla_{12}z_t = (1-0.64B)(1-0.68B^{12})a_t$ |
| Midlands (industry) | $\nabla\nabla_{12}z_t = (1-0.77B)(1-0.57B^{12})a_t$ |
| Midlands (company) | $\nabla\nabla_{12}z_t = (1-0.80B)(1-0.70B^{12})a_t$ |
| Scotland (industry) | $\nabla\nabla_{12}z_t = (1-0.84B)(1-0.35B^{12})a_t$ |
| Scotland (company) | $\nabla\nabla_{12}z_t = (1-0.62B)(1-0.60B^{12})a_t$ |

moving averages of data). This similarity has been found to occur quite frequently for groups of similar products, the common model structure reflecting the fact that the marketing environment is similar for each product;

(2) the parameter values are approximately the same for different regions, confirming that a single common model might be used for forecasting purposes (see below);

(3) the models for total industry sales and for company sales in each region are very similar, because of the approximate stability of the market share. However it was found necessary to introduce a system to monitor market share in one region, where there was greatest competition, since there was evidence that market share tended to drop with a fall in the level of total industry sales.

Prior to this study, forecasts were based on salesmen's reports and yielded forecast errors one month ahead with standard deviations approximately equal to 10% of average sales. Based on the models of Table 3, the standard deviations were reduced to approximately 5%.

Some care was taken to present the computer-generated forecasts to management in a simple way. Table 4 shows the layout for the forecasts that was eventually agreed with management. Where comparisons with actual sales were possible, the one-month-ahead forecast errors were displayed (See last column of Table 4). Based on the values of the standard deviations of the residuals obtained when the models were fitted, a warning signal was generated if a single forecast error, or a run of forecast errors, was abnormally large compared with its standard deviation.

Table 4

Layout of monthly computer print out of sales forecasts for one region from origin December 1969.

| Date | Sales forecasts | Sales last 12 months | Actual sales | One month-ahead forecast errors |
|------|-----------------|----------------------|--------------|--------------------------------|
| etc. | etc. | etc. | etc. | etc. |
| Sept. 69 | – | 2293 | 199 | 13.0 |
| Oct. 69 | – | 2320 | 217 | –0.5 |
| Nov. 69 | – | 2315 | 183 | –7.5 |
| Dec. 69 | – | 2280 | 151 | 22.0 |
| Jan. 70 | 155 | 2273 | – | – |
| Feb. 70 | 154 | 2290 | – | – |
| Mar. 70 | 216 | 2305 | – | – |
| Apr. 70 | 194 | 2304 | – | – |
| May 70 | 220 | 2313 | – | – |
| etc. | etc. | etc. | – | – |

For certain planning decisions (especially those associated with distribution), forecasts were needed for much smaller sales areas. Since there was a large number of sales areas, it was not feasible to develop a model for each such area. Hence the forecasts generated by the regional models of Table 3 were broken down into forecasts for individual sales areas using proportionality factors which depended on:

(a) the proportion of the regional sales contributed by a particular sales area in the previous year,

(b) recent market intelligence (e.g. a new customer is expected or an existing customer has won a new contract).

Figure 16 is a simplified diagram of how the forecast generating system was organised. It was found sufficient to update the models every 12 months, using the more recently available data and rejecting earlier data.

*On-line model adaption and monitoring.* More recent experience with problems of this kind has led to the following approach for situations where it is necessary to forecast as many as 500 products:

(1) the product range is divided into market segments,

(2) a few products are selected from each market segment and univariate models fitted to sales data for each such product,

(3) if there is evidence that a 'common model' structure can be used for a

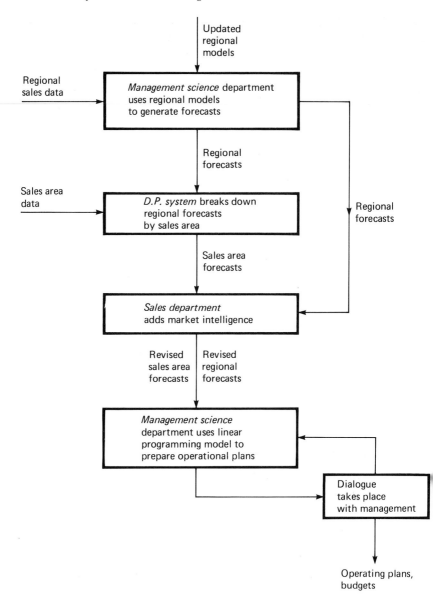

Fig 16. Simplified diagram showing how forecasts were used to generate operational plans for a company in the process industries.

particular market segment, the parameters for the common model are derived by averaging the parameter estimates for the few products analysed,

(4) the 'common model' is used to forecast the sales of each product in the market segment, as shown in Figure 17. Because the 'common model' is a compromise for all products, it will not necessarily be the best for a particular product. Hence the one-step-ahead forecast errors will not be random in general,

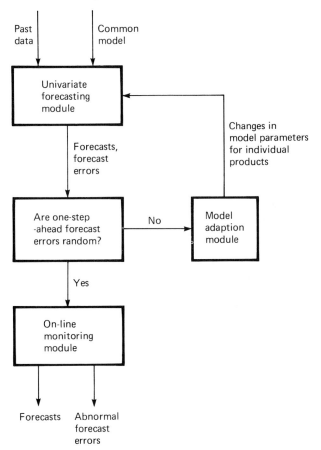

Fig 17. On-line model adaption and forecast monitoring system for handling a large number of products.

(5) if a test for the randomness of the one-step-ahead forecast errors indicates that correlation is present, a model adaption module (Figure 17) is used to modify the parameters in the 'common model' so as to suit the particular series at hand,

(6) if there is no evidence of non-randomness in the one-step-ahead forecast errors, either initially or after model adaption, the forecasts are printed out by the computer. However, as new data comes to hand the forecast errors are monitored and abnormal changes recorded – for example, a large forecast error, or a change in the mean of the forecast errors, has occurred at a particular point in time.

In this way, after the preliminary analysis has been undertaken, large numbers of time series can be handled on an automatic basis, with abnormal situations signalled on an *exception* basis, so that an investigation can be started as to the cause of the anomalies. Applications of this approach have been made not only in manufacturing industry but also in forecasting deposits and withdrawals on an area basis for banks.

## 3.2. *Three applications of transfer function models*

Three applications of transfer function modelling will be described:

(1) The relationship between Market Share, Relative Price and Relative Advertising for a *non-seasonal* consumer product,

(2) the relationship between Electricity Consumption and Temperature (both *seasonal* series) for a national economy,

(3) the relationship between Manufacturing Employment and Manufacturing Output for the Federal Republic of Germany using quarterly and annual data.

### 3.2.1. *Relationship between market share, price and advertising*

This analysis formed part of a wider study to investigate the effect of various advertising and pricing policies on a range of consumer products. The following analysis relates to one product only.

Figure 18 shows the structure of the model, which relates the output variable, Market Share $(Y_t)$ to two input variables: Relative Advertising $(X_{1t})$ and Relative Price $(X_{2t})$. Relative Advertising is defined as the ratio of the company's advertising on a consumer product to the total industry advertising on this particular type of product. Relative Price is the ratio of the company's price to a volume-weighted price for the industry.

Figure 19 shows time series data relating to the three variables in the model. The data series were recorded at intervals of four weeks for a period of 38 time intervals (nearly three years). Table 5 shows univariate models fitted to each time series separately.

The univariate model of the Market Share series is needed for two reasons:

(i) so that the reduction in residual variance, as a result of introducing the input variables $X_{1t}$ and $X_{2t}$, can be measured,

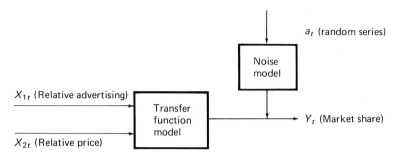

Fig 18. Structure of market share model relating market share $(Y_t)$ to relative advertising $(X_{1t})$ and relative price $(X_{2t})$.

(ii) to provide a first approximation to the structure of the noise model to be used in the transfer function model.

The univariate models of the two input variables are needed to calculate the prewhitened cross correlation function between Market Share and each of the input variables, as is now illustrated in the case of Relative Advertising. The univariate model for relative advertising:

$$(1 - 0.80B + 0.53B^2)\nabla X_{1t} = c + (1 - 0.77B)(1 - 0.76B^{13})\alpha_{1t}$$

converts the highly correlated relative advertising series $X_{1t}$ into an (approximately) random series $a_{1t}$. The identical operation

$$(1 - 0.80B + 0.53B^2)\nabla Y_t = c + (1 - 0.77B)(1 - 0.76B^{13})\beta_{1t}$$

is then applied to the Market Share Series $Y_t$, converting it into another time series $\beta_{1t}$ which will not be random in general. The prewhitened cross correlation function between Market Share and Relative Advertising (Figure 20b) is then defined as the cross correlation function between $\beta_{1t}$ and $\alpha_{1t}$. This function has a large positive value at lag zero and is small thereafter, implying that an increase in Relative Advertising during the present four week period increases market share in the same period but has no influence on market share in the following periods. This observation suggests that a simple relationship

$$Y_t = \omega_0 X_{1t} + N_t \tag{1}$$

can be postulated between Market Share and Relative Advertising, where $N_t$ is a

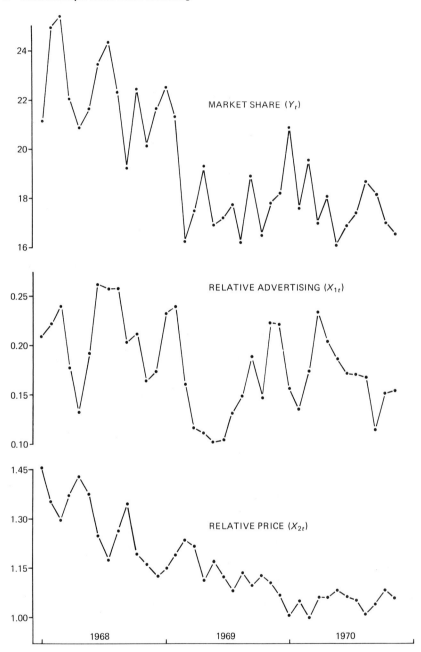

**Fig 19.** Market share, relative advertising and relative price of a consumer product: 4 week data from 1968, period 1 to 1970, period 12.

Table 5
Summary of univariate models fitted to each variable separately

| Variable | Fitted model | Residual variance |
|---|---|---|
| Market share | $\nabla Y_t = (1 - 0.63B)a_t$<br>$\pm 0.13$ | 3.30 |
| Relative advertising | $(1-0.80B + 0.53B^2)\nabla X_{1t} = -0.0017 + (1-0.77B)(1-0.76B^{13})\alpha_{1t}$<br>$\pm 0.15 \quad \pm 0.14 \qquad\qquad \pm 0.0014 \qquad \pm 0.14 \qquad \pm 0.08$ | 0.001103 |
| Relative price | $(1-0.41B)\nabla X_{2t} = -0.0053 + (1-0.95B)\alpha_{2t}$<br>$\pm 0.16 \qquad\qquad \pm 0.0008 \qquad \pm 0.15$ | 0.000819 |

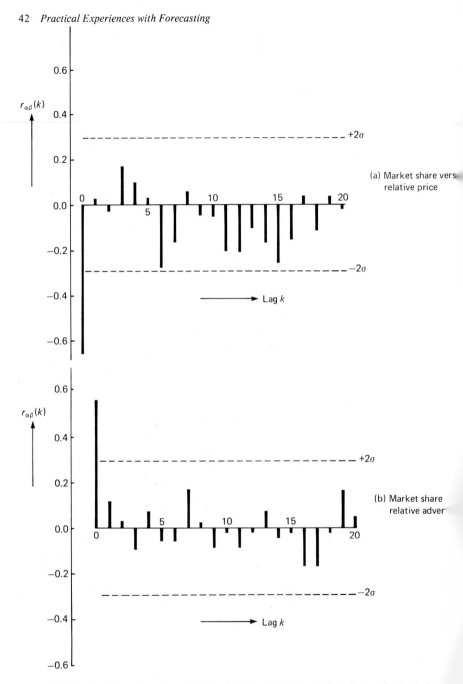

(a) Market share vers
relative price

(b) Market share
relative adver

Fig 20.  Prewhitened cross correlation functions between market share and (a) relative (b) relative advertising.

noise or error term. As a first approximation to the noise model $N_t$, we can take the univariate model for $Y_t$ given in Table 5, that is

$$\nabla N_t = (1 - \theta B)a_t \tag{2}$$

On combining (1) and (2), we obtain the transfer function-noise model

$$\nabla Y_t = \omega_0 \nabla X_{1t} + (1 - \theta B)a_t \tag{3}$$

in which $\omega_0$ and $\theta$ must now be estimated simultaneously. The justification for the use of the univariate model for $Y_t$ as a first approximation to the model for the noise $N_t$ is that if $\omega_0 = 0$ in (1), then $Y_t = N_t$. If $\omega_0 \neq 0$, as will be the case in this example, we are essentially fitting the transfer function model by perturbing about the univariate model. The fitted model is shown in the second row of Table 6.

Figure 20(a) shows the prewhitened cross correlation function between Market Share and Relative Price, using the univariate model for Relative Price given in Table 5. The cross correlation function has a large negative spike at lag zero and small correlations thereafter, suggesting a model with the same structure as the Relative Advertising model. The fitted model is shown in the third row of Table 6, from which it is seen that the residual variance is much smaller than for the Relative Advertising model, indicating that Relative Price has a much greater influence on Market Share than Relative Advertising.

A final model was fitted with both Relative Advertising and Relative Price as input variables. Because there is little correlation between $X_{1t}$ and $X_{2t}$, we can use as an initial guess of the structure of the two input model, the structures of the two single input models. The fitted two input model is shown in the last row of Table 6, all the parameters in the model being estimated simultaneously. It can be seen that there is a further reduction in the residual variance as compared with the single input models. The dominance of Relative Price is again apparent from the magnitude of the estimate of the price parameter, compared with its standard error, in relation to the magnitude of the Advertising parameter, compared with its standard error. The two-input model implies that a unit increase in Advertising increases Market Share by $7.9\% \pm 3.8\%$ and that a unit increase in price decreases Market Share by $40.5\% \pm 6.2\%$.

Manipulation of the two-input model in Table 6 enables it to be written in the alternative form

$$(Y_t - \bar{Y}_{t-1}) = 7.9(X_{1t} - \bar{X}_{1,t-1}) - 40.5(X_{2t} - \bar{X}_{2,t-1}) + a_t$$

Table 6
Summary of univariate and transfer function models relating market share $(Y_t)$ to relative advertising $(X_{1t})$ and relative price $(X_{2t})$

| Model type | Fitted Model | Residual Variance |
|---|---|---|
| Univariate (market share) | $\nabla Y_t = (1 - 0.63B)a_t$ <br> $\pm 0.13$ | 3.30 |
| Single input Transfer function (versus relative advertising) | $\nabla Y_t = 16.1\nabla X_{1t} + (1-0.65B)a_t$ <br> $\pm 5.3 \qquad \pm 0.15$ | 2.62 |
| Single input transfer function (versus relative price) | $\nabla Y_t = -44.5\nabla X_{2t} + (1-0.43B)a_t$ <br> $\pm 6.2 \qquad \pm 0.15$ | 1.29 |
| Two input transfer function (versus relative advertising and relative price) | $\nabla Y_t = 7.9\nabla X_{1t} - 40.5\nabla X_{2t}$ <br> $\pm 3.8 \qquad \pm 6.2$ <br> $+ (1 - 0.45B)a_t$ <br> $\pm 0.15$ | 1.08 |

where $\bar{Y}_{t-1}$, $\bar{X}_{1,t-1}$ and $\bar{X}_{2,t-1}$ are exponentially weighted moving averages with smoothing constant 0.45 and starting at time $t-1$. Thus, although the models of Table 6 look deceptively simple, containing few parameters, in effect they are quite sophisticated since they involve applying exponential smoothing to the three time series and then relating the smoothed series by what is effectively classical regression analysis with random residuals. Such smoothing is not arbitrarily chosen, of course, but is determined by the structure of the model as developed during the model building process.

In this application, the main objective was not to forecast as such but to gain an understanding of the mechanisms relating sales of various products to price and advertising expenditure. Based on models such as those in Table 6, an investigation can then be made of the effect of changes in price and advertising on market share, sales volume, sales revenue and profitability.

### 3.2.2. Relationship between electricity consumption and temperature

This section describes an application of transfer function modelling to the relationship between two seasonal time series: an output series $Y_t$ consisting of the monthly electricity consumption for a national economy and an input series $X_t$, consisting of the corresponding mean monthly temperatures. The latter were defined as the weighted average of the temperatures in five regions, the weights being proportional to the mean electricity consumption in a particular region. In this application greater emphasis will be placed on the technical aspects of the model building.

The upper part of Figure 21 shows a plot of the $Y_t$ and $X_t$ series and the lower part of Figure 21 their *range-mean plots*. This data provides an opportunity to emphasize another aspect of the identification stage (see Table 2 and Figures A.1, A.3) of the model building process, namely the transformation of the data before building a model. This is necessary because, in some situations, if no transformation is applied the variability of the residuals may increase with time, thus violating one of the assumptions made in the model. A rough indication of the nature of the transformation can be obtained by dividing the time series into sub-series and plotting the range against the mean for each sub-series (see Appendix A.1). The linear relationship between the range and mean of the electricity consumption series $Y_t$ suggests the need for a logarithmic transformation of this series whilst the random scatter present in the range-mean plot of the temperature series $X_t$ suggests that no transformation of this series is needed. Figure 22(a) shows the logarithms of the earlier part of the electricity consumption series together with the autocorrelation function of the whole series. The latter is characterised by a period of 12 and a failure to damp out, suggesting that the series is non-stationary and that nonseasonal differencing $\nabla \ln Y_t$ is needed. Figure 22(b) shows the series $\nabla \ln Y_t$ and its autocorrelation function. Whereas the differencing has removed the trend in the original series, seasonal non-stationarity is indicated by a failure to damp out at lags 12, 24, 36 etc. Indeed, the seasonal behaviour is more clearly visible than in the autocorrelation function of the original series. Thus, the need for further seasonal differencing $\nabla_{12}$ is demonstrated and Figure 22(c) shows the series $\nabla \nabla_{12} \ln Y_t$ and its autocorrelation function. The latter indicates that no further differencing is required and that the series $\nabla \nabla_{12} \ln Y_t$ is approximately stationary.

Figure 22(c) shows that the largest autocorrelations of $\nabla \nabla_{12} \ln Y_t$ occur at lags 1 and 12, suggesting that we may take as our initial guess of the structure of the model:

$$\nabla \nabla_{12} \ln Y_t = (1 - \theta B)(1 - \Theta B^{12}) a_t$$

Based on the first-lag autocorrelation $r_1 = -0.27$ of $\nabla \nabla_{12} \ln Y_t$, we may take $\hat{\theta} = 0.30$ as an initial estimate of $\theta$. Based on the twelfth-lag autocorrelation $r_{12} = -0.33$ of $\nabla \nabla_{12} \ln Y_t$, an initial estimate of $\hat{\Theta} = 0.35$ is suggested for $\Theta$ (see Box and Jenkins, 1970, pages 517, 518).

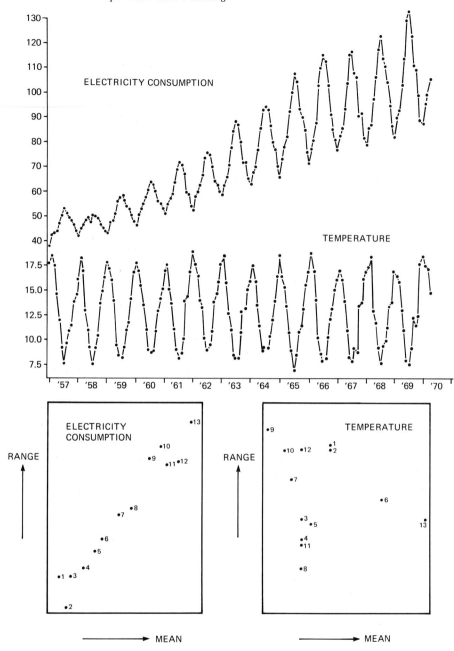

Fig 21. Plot of national electricity consumption and temperature, together with their range-mean plots: monthly data from January 1957 to April 1970. (Sub-series of 12 were used for calculation of range-mean plots; figure shows the sequence number of each sub-series).

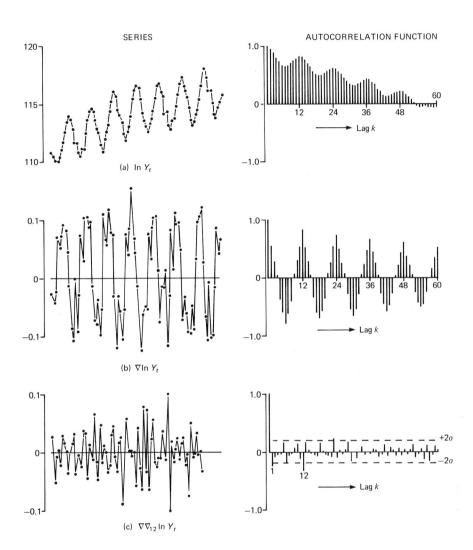

Fig 22. Various differences of electricity consumption series, together with their corresponding autocorrelation functions.

Table 7
Summary of univariate models fitted to national electricity consumption

| Data set | Estimated model | Residual variance (per cent s.d.) |
|---|---|---|
| Whole series ($N = 160$) | $\nabla\nabla_{12} \ln Y_t = (1-0.30B)(1-0.55B^{12})a_t$ <br> $\pm 0.08 \quad \pm 0.07$ | 0.0008010 (2.8%) |
| First half ($N = 64$) | $\nabla\nabla_{12} \ln Y_t = (1 + 0.14B)(1 - 0.83B^{12})a_t$ <br> $\pm 0.12 \quad \pm 0.04$ | 0.0005616 (2.4%) |
| Second half ($N = 96$) | $\nabla\nabla_{12} \ln Y_t = (1 - 0.73B)(1 - 0.83B^{12})a_t$ <br> $\pm 0.08 \quad \pm 0.05$ | 0.0006481 (2.55%) |

The fitted model, based on $N = 160$ monthly observations, is shown in the first row of Table 7. The estimate of the residual standard deviation $\hat{\sigma} = 0.0283$ has a simple interpretation when a logarithmic transformation has been applied, as in this case. On multiplying by 100 we obtain a value of 2.8% which implies that the standard deviation of the residuals is approximately 2.8% of the 'level' of the series. Stated another way, it implies that approximately 2 out of 3 of the forecast errors one-step-ahead resulting from the use of the model can be expected to be less than 2.8% (in absolute value) of the level of the series at any point.

Figure 23(a) shows the residuals $a_t$ and Figure 23(b) the residual autocorrelation function for the 'whole series' model. It can be seen that there are residual autocorrelations larger than two standard deviations at lags 6, 13, 23, 25, 29 and 31 and the corresponding chi-squared statistic (56.6 on approximately 30 degrees of freedom) corresponds to a probability level of approximately 0.002 under the assumption that the residual series is random, indicating model inadequacy. Further elaboration of the model by adding in turn non-seasonal and seasonal parameters did not result in a reduction in the size of these large residual autocorrelations. This state of affairs sometimes occurs with long time series. Whereas problems occur with short series because it may not be possible to obtain a satisfactory diagnosis of the structure of the model and accurate estimates of the parameters, the problem with longer series is different. With long series it may happen that changing circumstances cause the structure of the series to change slowly with time. To test this hypothesis, the series was split into approximately equal halves, the second half being somewhat longer than the first half in order to preserve a reasonable length of recent data to model for forecasting purposes. Table 7 shows the models fitted to the two halves

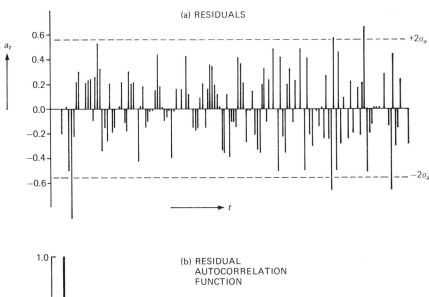

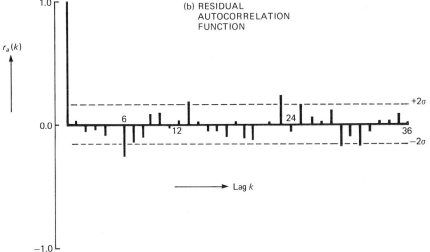

Fig 23. Residuals $a_t$ and residual autocorrelation function $r_a(k)$ for univariate model

$$\nabla\nabla_{12}\ln Y_t = (1 - 0.30B)(1 - 0.55B^{12})a_t$$

fitted to the whole series of electricity consumption ($N = 160$ observations).

separately. Whereas there is reasonable agreement between the estimates of the seasonal parameter for the two halves, there is clear evidence that the estimates of the non-seasonal parameter differ significantly from one half to the next. However, the residual autocorrelation functions for the two models fitted to each half separately do not display abnormal values, confirming that these models are representationally adequate. A possible explanation for this behaviour is that the $X$-series behaves differently as between the first and second half of the series. However, the behaviour of the temperature series is fairly regular and so this possibility can be ruled out. Accordingly, it was decided to work with the second half of the series for transfer function modelling.

*Prewhitening.* The modelling of the temperature series was relatively straight-forward and is not described in detail here. Since the temperature series does not contain a trend, no non-seasonal differencing was needed. However, since the temperature series is highly seasonal, seasonal differencing $\nabla_{12}$ was required. The final model was

$$(1 - 0.27B)\nabla_{12} X_t = (1 - 0.88B^{12})\alpha_t. \qquad (4)$$
$$\pm 0.08 \qquad\qquad \pm 0.03$$

Proceeding as in the example of Section 3.2.1, the prewhitened cross-correlation function is calculated by applying the temperature model (4) to the logarithm of the consumption series, that is

$$(1 - 0.27B)\nabla_{12}\ln Y_t = (1 - 0.88B^{12})\beta_t$$

and then calculating the cross-correlation function between $\beta_t$ and $\alpha_{t-k}$ at different lags $k$. Figure 24 shows the prewhitened series and the cross-correlation function, together with its approximate two standard error limits under the assumption that the two series are unrelated (see Box and Jenkins, 1970, p.376). The outstanding feature of the prewhitened cross correlation function is a large negative value at lag zero, implying that an increase in temperature this month decreases electricity consumption this month and vice versa. This behaviour suggests a relationship of the form

$$\ln Y_t = \omega_0 X_t + N_t \qquad (5)$$

between electricity consumption and temperature. As a first guess of the structure of the noise model we can use the univariate model for $\ln Y_t$ given in Table 7, namely

$$\nabla_{12}N_t = (1 - \theta B)(1 - \Theta B^{12})a_t. \qquad (6)$$

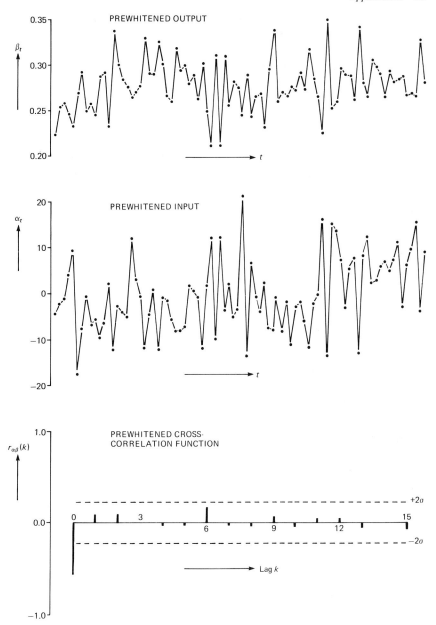

Fig 24. Prewhitened output (electricity consumption) series $\beta_t$, prewhitened input (temperature) series $\alpha_t$ and prewhitened cross correlation function $r_{\alpha\beta}(k)$.

Combining (5) and (6) we obtain for the overall transfer function-noise model.

$$\nabla\nabla_{12}\ln Y_t = \omega_0 \nabla\nabla_{12}X_t + (1 - \theta B)(1 - \Theta B^{12})a_t.$$

In addition to estimates of the prewhitened cross correlation function, the computer program MTID (see Appendix A.3) also calculates preliminary estimates of the *impulse response weights* $v_j$ in the impulse response representation*

$$\ln Y_t = v_0 X_t + v_1 X_{t-1} + v_2 X_{t-2} + \cdots + N_t \qquad (7)$$

relating $\ln Y_t$ and $X_t$. Comparing this representation with (5) above we see that an initial estimate of $\omega_0$ is provided by an estimate of $v_0$. In this example this was $v_0 = -0.0015$. Similarly, initial estimates of $\theta$ and $\Theta$ are obtained from the univariate model (based on $N = 96$) given in Table 7, namely $\hat{\theta} = 0.73$ and $\hat{\Theta} = 0.83$.

*Fitted transfer function model.* The final model, with $\omega_0$, $\theta$ and $\Theta$ estimated simultaneously by fully efficient likelihood methods is shown in Table 8, together with the best univariate model for comparison. The estimate of $\omega_0$ is approximately 10 times its standard error and there is a very large reduction in residual variance as compared with the univariate model. Written in the form

$$\ln Y_t = -0.00222 X_t + N_t$$
$$\pm 0.00020$$

where

$$\nabla\nabla_{12} N_t = (1 - 0.64B)(1 - 0.75B^{12})a_t$$
$$\pm 0.09 \qquad \pm 0.09$$

the model is capable of a simple interpretation. It implies that a $1°$ Centigrade rise in temperature in a given month decreases electricity consumption by $0.22\% \pm 0.02\%$ in that same month.

---

*As a starting point in the identification of the lag structure, it is convenient to assume that there is a parameter $v_j$, called the impulse response weight, associated with each lag. The prewhitened cross correlation when multiplied by a constant provides estimates of the impulse response weights $v_j$, and hence can be used to suggest a more parsimonious representation of the lag structure based on a few parameters — which can then be estimated efficiently.

Table 8
Comparison of univariate and transfer function models fitted to second half ($N = 96$) of electricity consumption ($Y_t$) and temperature ($X_t$) series.

| Model type | Estimated model | Residual Variance (% s.d.) |
|---|---|---|
| Univariate | $\nabla\nabla_{12} \ln Y_t = (1 - 0.74B)(1 - 0.83B^{12})a_t$ <br> $\quad\quad\pm0.08 \quad\quad \pm0.05$ | 0.0006481 <br> (2.55%) |
| Transfer function | $\nabla\nabla_{12} \ln Y_t = -0.00222\nabla\nabla_{12}X_t$ <br> $\quad\quad\quad\pm0.00020$ <br> $\quad + (1 - 0.64B)(1 - 0.75B^{12})a_t$ <br> $\quad\quad\quad\pm0.09 \quad\quad \pm0.09$ | 0.0003032 <br> (1.74%) |

*Correlations between parameter estimates.* Another important aspect of an estimation situation is the *correlation matrix* of the parameter estimates. High correlations between parameter estimates indicate that the likelihood surface is elongated in certain directions, implying that there are many combinations of the parameters in the neighbourhood of the maximum likelihood estimates with very nearly equal likelihood. Such ambiguity in the estimation situation is undesirable and sometimes indicates that the model is too elaborate or that it is mis-specified. By the latter is meant that, for example, several autoregressive parameters may have been introduced into the model whereas fewer moving average parameters would have sufficed. When all attempts to remove high correlations have failed, it may be necessary to live with them, recognising that they are a property of the particular data set being analysed and a consequence of one's inability to *design experiments* to collect time series data with the objective of achieving uncorrelated (orthogonal) parameter estimates.

The correlation matrix of the three parameters in the transfer function model of Table 8 is shown below.

|  | $\hat{\omega}_0$ | $\hat{\theta}$ | $\hat{\Theta}$ |
|---|---|---|---|
| $\hat{\omega}_0$ | 1.00 | | |
| $\hat{\theta}$ | 0.14 | 1.00 | |
| $\hat{\Theta}$ | 0.00 | −0.07 | 1.00 |

It is rather remarkable that what, at first sight, seems a rather complex relationship between two series can be described by a model containing only three parameters and that these parameters are virtually orthognal.

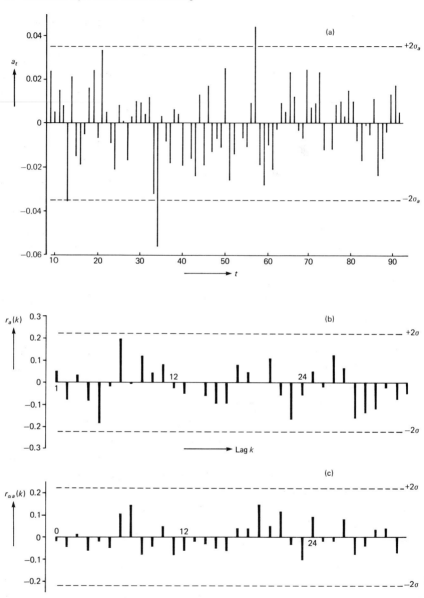

Fig 25. Diagnostic checks for transfer function model relating electricity consumption to temperature: (a) residuals $a_t$, (b) residual autocorrelation function $r_a(k)$, (c) cross-correlation function $r_{\alpha a}(k)$ between residuals and prewhitened temperature series.

Figure 25 shows the residuals $a_t$ from the transfer function model given in Table 8, the autocorrelation function $r_a(k)$ of the residuals and the cross-correlation function $r_{\alpha a}(k)$ between the residuals and the prewhitened temperature. There is no obvious evidence of model inadequacy. However, there are two large consecutive residuals at $t = 38$ $(-1.9\sigma_a)$ and $t = 39$ $(-3.3\sigma_a)$ but no explanation could be found for these.

The nature of the checks shown in Figure 25 should be noted:

(1) A plot of the residuals $a_t$ (Figure 25(a)), together with 'control limits' $\pm 2\sigma_a$, can indicate points where the residuals seem to be unrepresentative, when compared with the overall distribution of residuals. Such unrepresentative, or abnormal, residuals are indicative of large external shocks, such as a strike or, quite often, an anomaly in the data due to misrecording or wrong transcription.

(2) The residual autocorrelation function (Figure 25(b)) looks for evidence of non-randomness in the residuals. Such non-randomness could be indicative of inadequacies in the transfer function model and the noise model. (See Box and Jenkins, 1970, pages 392, 393).

(3) The cross correlation function between the residuals and the temperature series (Figure 25(c)) provides evidence of inadequacy in the transfer function model. (see Box and Jenkins, 1970, pages 393, 394).

Most econometric models quote as evidence of the 'adequacy' the Durbin–Watson (DW) statistic (see Durbin and Watson, 1950, 1951). Whereas this statistic has served a useful purpose in the past, it should be remembered that it is equivalent to the first lag of the residual autocorrelation function. Thus, a model could be inadequate despite an 'acceptable' Durbin–Watson statistic, due to the presence of large autocorrelations at lags greater than 1. More importantly, even if the residual autocorrelations are satisfactory, the model could still be unsatisfactory since significant cross-correlations might exist between the residuals and the 'independent variables'. Such cross correlation checks are very important since they provide clues as to the inadequacy of the transfer function. The absence of such checks from econometric models represents a serious deficiency in the building of such models.

*Forecasting.* The transfer function model forecasts of electricity consumption can be calculated only if there exist forecasts of temperature for various lead times. Table 9a and Figure 26 show forecasts of the electricity consumption series for lead times $1, 2, \ldots, 12$ months from origin $t = 96$, based on:

(a) the univariate model of Table 8,

(b) the transfer function model of Table 8, with temperature forecast using

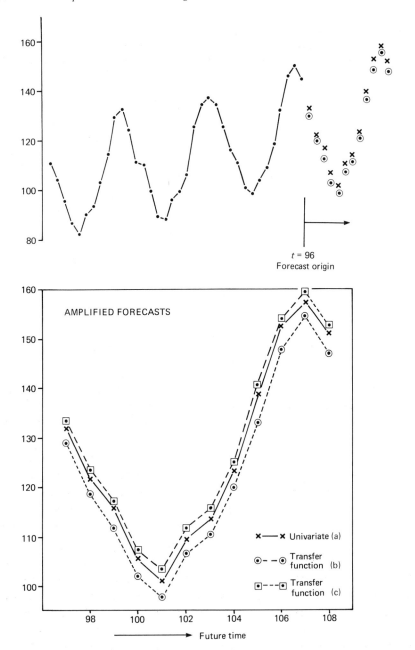

Fig 26. Forecasts of electricity consumption for lead times 1, 2, . . . , 12 from origin *t* = 96, based on (a) univariate model, transfer function model with temperature forecast (b) from its univariate model, (c) from its univariate model less 5%.

Table 9a
Three forecasts of electricity consumption for lead times 1, 2, . . . , 12, from origin
$t$ = 96, based on (a) univariate model for electricity consumption, (b) transfer function,
based on univariate model forecast of temperature, (c) transfer function, based on univariate
model of temperature, less 5%.

| Observation number | (1) Univariate electricity forecast | (2) Univariate temperature forecast | (3) Transfer function electricity forecast using (2) | (4) Temperature forecast (2) less 5% | (5) Transfer function electricity forecast using (4) |
|---|---|---|---|---|---|
| 97  | 129.1 | 11.0 | 132.0 | 10.4 | 133.6 |
| 98  | 118.8 | 12.4 | 121.8 | 11.7 | 123.5 |
| 99  | 111.9 | 13.7 | 115.6 | 13.0 | 117.3 |
| 100 | 102.2 | 15.9 | 105.5 | 15.1 | 107.4 |
| 101 | 97.7  | 17.0 | 101.6 | 16.1 | 103.6 |
| 102 | 106.7 | 17.6 | 109.6 | 16.7 | 111.7 |
| 103 | 110.4 | 16.5 | 113.6 | 15.7 | 115.7 |
| 104 | 119.9 | 13.7 | 123.4 | 13.0 | 125.3 |
| 105 | 135.6 | 11.4 | 138.8 | 10.8 | 140.6 |
| 106 | 147.8 | 9.1  | 152.5 | 8.6  | 154.0 |
| 107 | 154.6 | 8.6  | 157.3 | 7.9  | 159.5 |
| 108 | 147.0 | 9.4  | 151.1 | 9.0  | 152.7 |

the univariate model (4) for temperature,

(c) the transfer function model of Table 8, with the temperature forecasts set
to be those obtained from the univariate temperature model (4), less 5%.

Table 9b compares the standard deviations of the forecast errors at various
lead times, implied by different models and assumptions. The standard deviations are expressed as per cent standard deviations in order to make their
interpretation easier. Column 1 of Table 9b shows the standard deviations of the
forecast errors at different lead times for the univariate model (Assumption (a)).
Column 2 shows the corresponding standard deviations for the transfer function
model when the temperature series is forecast using its univariate model
(Assumption (b)). It is seen that although the transfer function model has a
much smaller residual standard deviation than the univariate model, (see Table
8), its forecasting performance is not markedly better because of the inaccur-
acies in forecasting the temperature series. However, this is to take a very
pessimistic view concerning the forecasting of temperature. Column 3 shows the
standard deviations of the forecast errors when it is assumed that future values
of the temperature series *are known exactly* (as in assumption (c)). This, of
course, is to take a very optimistic point of view. In practice, a good forecaster,

Table 9b
Per cent standard deviations of forecast errors of electricity consumption at various lead times, based on different models and forecasts

| Lead time | Univariate model | Transfer function model (temperature forecast) | Transfer function model (temperature known) |
|:---:|:---:|:---:|:---:|
| 1 | 2.55 | 2.49 | 1.72 |
| 2 | 2.63 | 2.62 | 1.84 |
| 3 | 2.71 | 2.70 | 1.95 |
| 4 | 2.79 | 2.78 | 2.06 |
| 5 | 2.87 | 2.86 | 2.16 |
| 6 | 2.94 | 2.93 | 2.25 |
| 7 | 3.02 | 3.00 | 2.35 |
| 8 | 3.09 | 3.07 | 2.44 |
| 9 | 3.16 | 3.14 | 2.52 |
| 10 | 3.23 | 3.21 | 2.60 |
| 11 | 3.30 | 3.27 | 2.68 |
| 12 | 3.36 | 3.34 | 2.76 |
| 13 | 3.54 | 3.51 | 2.96 |
| 14 | 3.62 | 3.60 | 3.07 |
| 15 | 3.70 | 3.69 | 3.17 |
| 16 | 3.78 | 3.78 | 3.27 |
| 17 | 3.86 | 3.87 | 3.37 |
| 18 | 3.94 | 3.95 | 3.47 |

exploiting the judgement of meteorological experts should be able to do better than the supine forecast implied by Column 2. Hence, a desirable practical objective would be to try and achieve a performance intermediate between Columns 2 and 3.

The above situation represents a fairly simple example of energy forecasting. It forms part of a wider range of experience of modelling and forecasting electricity, gas, coal and petroleum products. These exercises have not only involved single-input models relating energy consumption to temperature but also multiple-input models involving temperature, a measure of economic activity (such as G.D.P. or an index of Manufacturing Production) and price variables. Such models have been based on daily, weekly, monthly, quarterly and annual data and have been used for short term operational planning (forecasts of tomorrow's energy consumption for optimising grid distribution), medium term planning (up to 24 months ahead for scheduling capacity and pricing decisions) and longer term planning (2–7 years ahead for investment planning).

### 3.2.3. *Relationships between manufacturing employment, G.D.P. and manufacturing output*

As a simple illustration of the application of transfer function modelling to macro-economic time series, in this section we consider the relationship between Manufacturing Employment $(Y_t)$ and various measures of economic Output $(X_t)$ for the Federal Republic of Germany (West Germany). These analyses form part of a much wider study concerned with the forecasting of employment in 12 different sectors for each of the 9 countries in the European Common Market.

Two different types of model will be described:

(a) A relationship between Manufacturing Employees (total employment less the self-employed) and Manufacturing Output, based on *quarterly* (seasonally unadjusted) data,

(b) a relationship between Manufacturing Employment (including self-employed persons) and Gross Domestic Product (G.D.P.), based on *annual* data.

*(a) Quarterly model.* Figure 27 shows quarterly data for Manufacturing Employees $(Y_t)$ and Manufacturing Output $(X_t)$ in West Germany for the period 1963, Quarter 4 to 1974, Quarter 4. The quarterly Manufacturing Employees series is published by the Deutsches Institut für Wirtschaftsforschung and excludes self-employed persons. The Manufacturing Output series is an index of production for the manufacturing industries (published by SOEC).

The univariate model for Manufacturing Employment was

$$(1 - 1.20B + 0.39B^2)\nabla\nabla_4 \ln Y_t = (1 - 0.69B^4)a_t \qquad (8)$$
$$\pm 0.15 \quad \pm 0.16 \qquad\qquad\qquad \pm 0.11$$

with residual variance $\sigma_a^2 = 0.3528 \times 10^{-4}$. As explained previously, because the model is based on the natural logarithms of employment, the residual standard deviation $\sigma_a = 0.00594$ has a particularly simple interpretation. It implies that the standard deviation of the residuals unexplained by the model, or alternatively the standard deviation of the one-quarter-ahead forecast errors, is 0.59% of the level of the forecast. The operator $(1 - 1.20B + 0.39B^2)$ in the model also has an interesting interpretation. This operator is complex and its period $p$, given by

$$\cos\left(\frac{2\pi}{p}\right) = \frac{\phi_1}{2\sqrt{-\phi_2}} = \frac{1.20}{2\sqrt{0.39}}$$

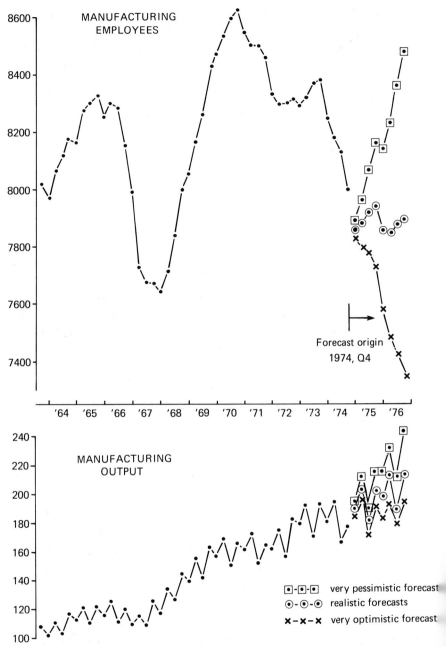

Fig 27. Manufacturing employees (000's) and index of manufacturing output for the Federal Republic of Germany: quarterly data from 1963, quarter 4 to 1974, quarter 4; forecasts of manufacturing employees based on (1) a very pessimistic forecast, (2) a realistic forecast, (3) a very optimistic forecast, of manufacturing output.

(See Box and Jenkins 1970 p.260), is equal to 22.3 quarters or 5.6 years. This period corresponds to the 'business cycle' in the Employees series. Unlike other methods of describing cycles, the autoregressive operator $1 - \phi_1 B - \phi_2 B^2$ in the model is capable of describing cyclical phenomena containing not *fixed* periods but ones which are subject to random changes in period, amplitude and phase, as governed by the random series $a_t$ in the model.

Based on a univariate model for Manufacturing Output,

$$(1 - 0.25B)(1 + 0.21B^4 + 0.51B^8)\nabla\nabla_4 \ln X_t = \alpha_t \tag{9}$$

the prewhitened cross correlation function was calculated and used to identify a transfer function model. The final model after two iterations of fitting and checking was

$$\ln Y_t = \frac{\overset{\pm 0.0193 \quad \pm 0.18}{0.1406\,(1 + 0.76B)}}{\underset{\pm 0.03}{(1 - 0.69B)}} \ln X_t + N_t \tag{10}$$

where the structure of the noise model $N_t$ was initially taken to be the same as the univariate model (8) for Manufacturing Employment. However, the noise model simplified during the model building process to

$$\nabla\nabla_4 N_t = \underset{\pm 0.16}{(1 - 0.40B^4)}a_t \tag{11}$$

On eliminating $N_t$ between (10) and (11), the overall transfer function-noise model is

$$\nabla\nabla_4 \ln Y_t = \frac{\overset{\pm 0.0193 \quad \pm 0.18}{0.1406(1 + 0.76B)}}{\underset{\pm 0.03}{(1 - 0.69B)}} \nabla\nabla_4 \ln X_t + \underset{\pm 0.16}{(1 - 0.40B^4)}a_t \tag{12}$$

with residual variance $\sigma_a^2 = 0.1413 \times 10^{-4}$. In (12) the parameters in the transfer function and noise parts of the model were fitted *simultaneously* using likelihood methods. The components (10) and (11) of the model are displayed here merely for ease of interpretation.

The following comments may be made concerning model (12):

(i) The residual variance $\sigma_a^2 = 0.1413 \times 10^{-4}$ is much smaller than the residual variance $\sigma_a^2 = 0.3528 \times 10^{-4}$ of the univariate model, indicating that Manufacturing Output is an important explanatory variable for forecasting

Manufacturing Employees, as is well known.

(ii) The noise structure in (12) is considerably simpler than the univariate model in (8). In particular, the autoregressive operator $(1 - 1.20B + 0.39B^2)$ in (8), which describes the business cycle in the Employees series, has disappeared in the transfer function model (12). Its role has now been taken over by the Manufacturing Output series $X_t$, which also reflects the business cycle.

(iii) The transfer function

$$\ln Y_t = \frac{0.1406(1 + 0.76B)}{(1 - 0.69B)} \ln X_t$$

in (10) may be interpreted as follows:

— on setting $B = 1$ in the transfer function, we obtain the gain

$$g = \frac{0.1406 (1 + 0.76)}{(1 - 0.69)} = 0.80.$$

In general, the gain measures the *ultimate* change (after the dynamic effects have subsided) in the output as a result of a unit change in an input. In this particular case it implies that a 1% increase in Manufacturing Output in a given quarter will *eventually* (after a time lag) increase Manufacturing Employment by 0.80%. The standard error of this gain may be calculated from a knowledge of the variances and covariances of the three parameter estimates in the transfer function and is ±0.08%.

— The transfer function may be expanded in the form

$$\ln Y_t = 0.1406(1 + 0.76B) \{1 + (0.69B) + (0.69B)^2 + (0.69B)^3 + \ldots\} \ln X_t$$

$$= (0.1406 + 0.2308B + 0.1406B^2 + 0.0972B^3 + 0.0671B^4 + \ldots) \ln X_t$$

implying that a 1% increase in Manufacturing Output this quarter will produce a

        0.14% increase in Employment this quarter,

        0.23% increase in the next quarter,

        0.14% increase in the next following quarter,

and so on. The sum of these contributions will be the gain 0.80%, as quoted above.

(iv) Only three parameters are needed to describe the lag structure in the transfer function and only one parameter is needed to describe the seasonal pattern in the noise or error left over after the effect of the seasonal Manufacturing Output series has been allowed for. This representation is a further example of the principle of parsimony and contrasts with many econometric models which suffer from over parameterisation.

(v) The transfer function-noise model describes the seasonality and lag structure under the umbrella of *one model*. This is in contrast to conventional approaches where input and output series are usually seasonally adjusted before fitting a relationship between them. Such seasonal adjustment methods are arbitrary (in the sense that a definition of a unique seasonal component is not possible), inflexible (in the sense that they apply a similar approach to all time series, irrespective of the characteristics of the series) and, in general, lead to a worsening in forecast accuracy. These criticisms do not imply that seasonal adjustment methods are not useful. On the contrary, after a model such as (12) above has been fitted, they can be useful in interpreting the model and the forecasts, as has been done for the telephone installations series in Figure 6 — but in this case the seasonal decomposition is determined by the structure of the model and not by a preset formula.

It should also be mentioned that the increasing tendency to publish seasonally adjusted series and to quote them in newspapers and on television tends to cause confusion in the minds of both technical people and lay people.*

(vi) To illustrate the sensitivity of Employment to changes in Output, Figure 27 shows forecasts of Manufacturing Employees for lead times 1, 2, ..., 8 quarters, based on three different assumptions about the future course of Manufacturing Output:

    (1) a very pessimistic assumption,

    (2) a realistic assumption,

    (3) a very optimistic assumption.

It is interesting to quote the model corresponding to (12) for the relationship between quarterly U.K. Manufacturing Employees and Manufacturing Output during the same period. This was

$$\nabla\nabla_4 \ln Y_t = \frac{\overset{\pm 0.025}{0.0839}}{\underset{\pm 0.05}{(1 - 0.82B)}} \nabla\nabla_4 \ln X_t - \underset{\pm 0.0043}{0.0700} \nabla\nabla_4 \xi_t + \frac{\overset{\pm 0.13}{(1 - 0.87B^4)}}{\underset{\pm 0.16 \quad \pm 0.15}{(1 - 0.12B - 0.27B^2)}} a_t$$

$$(13)$$

*A recent satirical cartoon illustrates the point well. The cartoon portrays an *unemployed* factory worker being interviewed by a television reporter. On being asked "Excuse me, sir, are you unemployed?", the factory worker replied, "No not really, I am just one of the seasonally adjusted ones"!

with residual variance $\sigma_a^2 = 0.2347 \times 10^{-4}$ (0.47 per cent standard deviation). In (13), $\xi_t$ is a unit step function starting at 1971, Quarter 3, an intervention variable introduced to allow for a change in definition of the method for counting Employees. The gain of the model (13) is $g = 0.47$, much smaller than that for the West German model (12). In the range of such models, fitted for most countries in the European Common Market, the gain for the U.K. model was intermediate in value between an essentially zero gain for Italy (implying a reluctance to make people unemployed during a fall in Output) and a high gain for West Germany (reflecting a sensitive response by Employment to rises and falls in Output).

*(b) Annual model.* Because of the difficulties involved in obtaining quarterly data for Manufacturing Employment data, which was only available for employees (total employment less the self employed) for many sectors of the E.E.C. economies, it became necessary to work with annual data, which was generally available for total employment (including the self employed). As an example, Figure 28 shows annual data for West Germany for the period 1960 to 1974. The variables plotted in Figure 28 are Manufacturing Employment $(Y_t)$ and G.D.P. $(X_t)$. The univariate model for Manufacturing Employment was:

$$\nabla \ln Y_t = \frac{1}{\underset{\pm 0.19 \quad \pm 0.19}{(1 - 0.30B + 0.69B^2)}} \, a_t \tag{14}$$

with $\sigma_a^2 = 1.37 \times 10^{-4}$ (per cent standard deviation = 1.85%). The model (14) has an autoregressive operator with average period 5.5 years corresponding to the business cycle. It is also characterised by two large residuals at 1967 $(-2.4\sigma_a)$ and at 1974 $(-2.2\sigma_a)$ corresponding to recessions in the economy — effects which should be explained by the transfer function model.

The transfer function model relating Manufacturing Employment to G.D.P. was

$$\nabla \ln Y_t = \underset{\pm 0.049 \quad \pm 0.050}{(0.842 + 0.472B)}(\nabla \ln X_t - 0.0368) + \underset{\pm 0.0005}{0.0016} + \frac{1}{\underset{\pm 0.26 \quad \pm 0.26}{(1 + 0.63B + 0.82B^2)}} a_t \tag{15}$$

with $\sigma_a^2 = 0.673 \times 10^{-4}$ and per cent standard deviation 1.34%. The transfer function model (15) is interesting in that:

(i) it demonstrates that effective models can sometimes be built with as few as 14 observations,

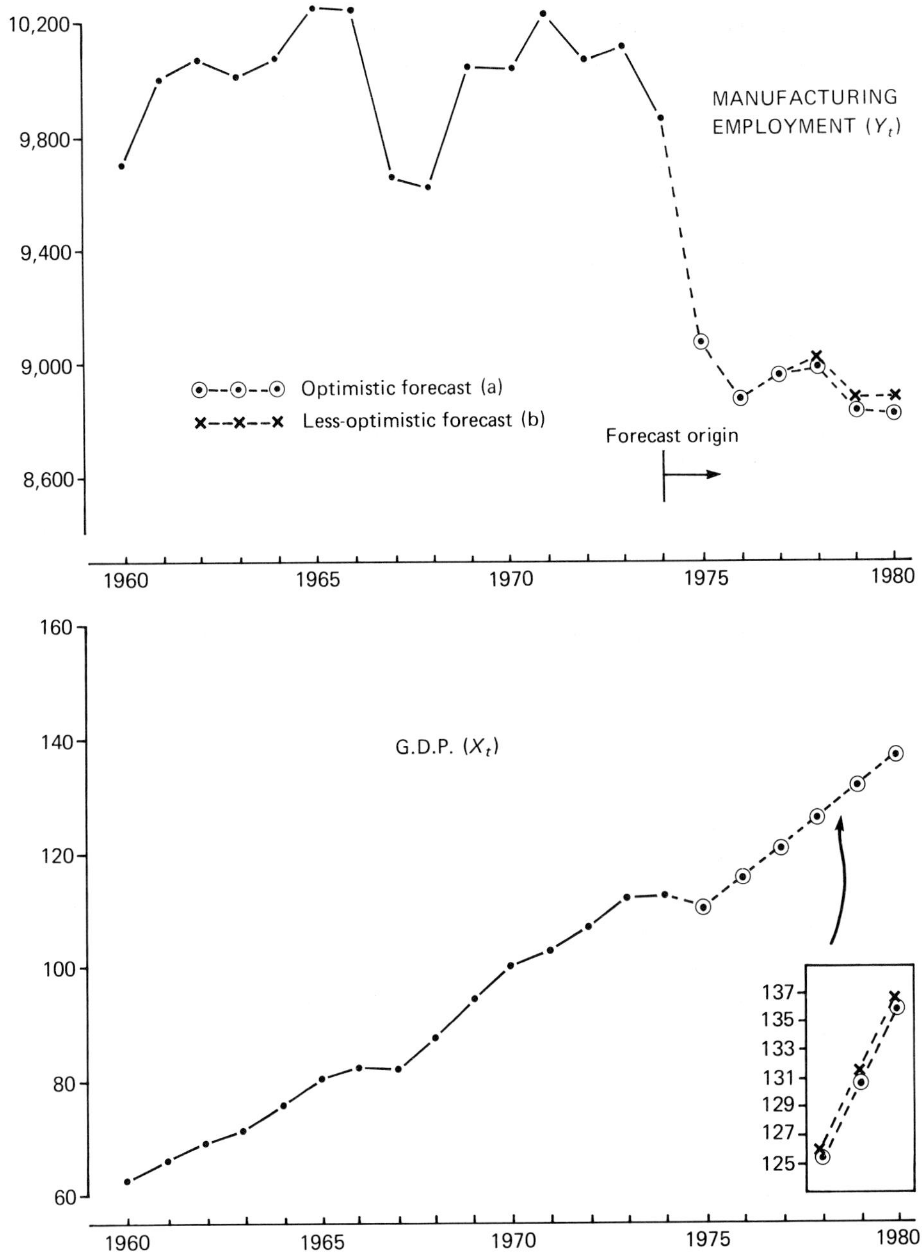

Fig 28. Manufacturing employment $(Y_t)$ and G.D.P. $(X_t)$ for West Germany: annual data from 1960–1974. Forecasts of manufacturing employment for lead times 1, ..., 6 years from origin 1974 based on: (a) optimistic forecast of G.D.P., (b) less-optimistic forecast of G.D.P.

(ii) there is a significant reduction in residual standard deviation as compared with the univariate model (14),

(iii) even after allowing for the constant growth rate component 0.0368 of G.D.P. (corresponding to an average growth rate of 3.68%), there remains a constant term 0.0016 (corresponding to an annual growth rate of 0.16%) in the model not explained by G.D.P. Possible explanations of this 'residual constant' are 'productivity changes' or 'technological changes' and they are of considerable interest in the investigation of employment changes,

(iv) the large residuals at 1967 and 1974 in the univariate model, and noted above, have disappeared in the transfer function model due to the introduction of G.D.P. as an explanatory variable,

(v) the gain of the model is $g = 1.3 \pm 0.1$, implying that a 1% increase in G.D.P. ultimately, after a lag of one year, increases Manufacturing Employment (but not, of course, employment in the whole of the economy) by $1.3\% \pm 0.1\%$,

(vi) Despite the introduction of G.D.P. into the model the noise term in (15) contains an autoregressive operator with an average period of 3.3 years.

Figure 28 shows forecasts of employment corresponding to two different forecasts of G.D.P.:

(a)  an optimistic forecast

(b)  a pessimistic forecast.

As in conventional econometric work, the above analysis assumes that there is a uni-directional relationship between G.D.P. and Employment. To first-order approximation, this is the case in this example. However, at the time of writing, this study (which is concerned with the forecasting of Employment in 12 sectors of the economies of each of the 9 countries in the European Economic Community) has been extended to include other variables such as Imports, Exports, Average Earnings and Investment, allowing the possibility for more complex relationships than those discussed in this section.

## 3.3. Two applications of intervention models

As explained in Section 2.3, abnormal events, such as strikes, policy changes and holidays, can sometimes distort the behaviour of a series, causing large residuals in the model. These large residuals can distort the identification of the model from the appropriate correlation or cross correlation function. They can also distort the values of the parameter estimates because the anomalous residuals exercise an excessively large weight in the calculation of the likelihood function.

Two examples of intervention analysis will be described in this section:

(i) the effect of a change in policy on bad debt collection,

(ii) the effects of various types of promotional activity on the sales of a consumer product.

### 3.3.1.   The effect of a change in policy on bad debt collection

The analysis presented here was part of a wider study concerned with the forecasting of outstanding debts for an international company. The present example concerns the forecasting of bad debt collection. Figure 29 shows a monthly series consisting of the bad debts collected in a major geographical area, together with a 30-day indicator which consists of the debts outstanding at the end of each month.

The first two rows of Table 10 show univariate and transfer function models developed for this data. It is seen that the introduction of the 30-day indicator results in a big reduction in the residual variance, as compared with the univariate model. Figure 30(a) shows the residuals $a_t$ from the transfer function model. There is a large positive residual in December 1974 followed by a run of negative residuals in the early months of 1975. Discussion of this anomalous behaviour with the organisation concerned revealed that a change in policy in relation to debt collection had taken place, more severe restrictions being placed on the granting of credit. However, when this new credit policy was announced at the end of 1974, there was a rush to take advantage of the more lenient credit facilities whilst they lasted. This resulted not only in a temporary increase in outstanding debt but also in an increase in debt collected, explaining the large residual in December 1974. From January 1975 onwards, there was a significant drop in the level of outstanding debt and in the debt collected each month.

Since these disturbances in the development of the series were *known* to have occurred, their effects were removed by introducing the following intervention variables:

(i) the effect due to anticipation of the change in policy in December 1974 was represented by a *pulse*

$$\xi_{1t} = \begin{cases} 1, & \text{December 1974,} \\ 0, & \text{otherwise.} \end{cases}$$

(ii) the change in policy in January 1975, was represented by a *step*

$$\xi_{2t} = \begin{cases} 0, & t < \text{January 1975,} \\ 1, & t \geqslant \text{January 1975.} \end{cases}$$

Fig 29. Bad debt collected each month and a leading indicator consisting of the total outstanding bad debt: monthly data from December 1972 to June 1975 ($N = 31$ observations).

The last row in Table 10 shows the effect of building these two intervention variables into the transfer function model. The model may be interpreted by writing it as follows:

$$Y_t = 0.70\, X_{t-1} + 13.2\, \xi_{1t} - 10.6\, \xi_{2t} + N_t \qquad (16)$$

where the noise $N_t$ is given by

$$\nabla N_t = a_t - 0.75\, a_{t-1}.$$

Thus, the amount of debt collected in month $t$ is explained by:

(i) multiplying the total debt outstanding in the previous month by 0.7,

(ii) a component of 13.2 units which represents the additional debt collected in December, 1974 above what might have been expected because of the anticipation of the new policy introduced in January 1975,

(iii) a drop in the mean level of 10.6 units from January, 1975 onwards due to the change in credit policy,

(iv) a noise or error term which describes the correlation between neighbouring months.

Table 10
Summary of models fitted to bad debt series.

| Model type | Estimated model | Residual variance (standard deviation) |
|---|---|---|
| Univariate | $\nabla Y_t = (1 - 0.41B)a_t$ <br> $\pm 0.17$ | 86.65 <br> (9.31) |
| Transfer function | $\nabla Y_t = 0.97 \nabla X_{t-1} + (1 - 0.69B)a_t$ <br> $\pm 0.11 \qquad\qquad \pm 0.14$ | 29.49 <br> (5.43) |
| Transfer function + intervention | $\nabla Y_t = 0.70 \nabla X_{t-1} + 13.2 \nabla \xi_{1t}$ <br> $\pm 0.08 \qquad\quad \pm 3.4$ <br><br> $\quad - 10.6 \nabla \xi_{2t} + (1 - 0.75B)a_t$ <br> $\quad\ \pm 3.1 \qquad\qquad \pm 0.13$ | 11.28 <br> (3.36) |

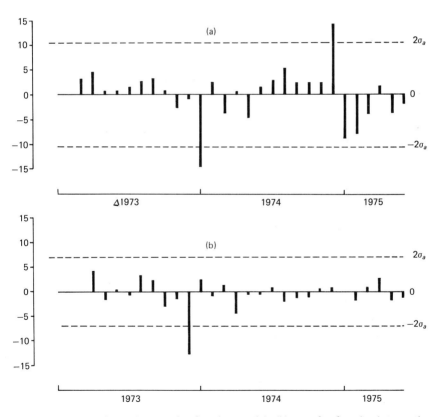

Fig 30. Residuals from: (a) transfer function model, (b) transfer function-intervention model fitted to the bad debt series.

Table 10 indicates that a dramatic reduction in the residual variance has taken place as a result of introducing the intervention variables. It illustrates the extent to which a few large residuals can distort a model.

In the above example, the intervention variables have been introduced into a transfer function model, converting it from a one-input model to a three-input model. Such intervention variables can be introduced into any of the four classes of model illustrated in Part 2. *But* it is a device that should be used only if there is evidence *external to the data* that an abnormal event has taken place. It should not be used as a device for removing residuals that are large and for which no reasonable explanation can be found.

Again, it should be emphasised that although the final model in Table 10 appears at first sight to be simple, it describes a large number of effects simultaneously. In addition to containing an indicator variable partially explaining the variable being forecast and a noise structure explaining correlation between neighbouring months, it also accounts for a permanent change in the level of the series. As such, intervention models represent generalisations of methods used for the analysis of data, usually not expressed as time series, and referred to by statisticians under the general title, 'The Design and Analysis of Experiments'.

### 3.3.2.  *The effects of promotional activity on sales of a consumer product*

This example formed part of a wider study to investigate the effects of various forms of promotional activity, price and advertising on the sales of certain consumer products. It is typical of a significant body of work carried out in this area over the past few years.

The data used for this illustration is given in Figure 31(a) and relates to 13 accounting periods during a year. Shown on the diagram are the 'normalised' sales data, together with two other series representing the periods when 'trade' and 'consumer' promotional activity took place. Because the number of delivery days per period varied between 18 and 25, the data was first 'normalised' by dividing by the number of delivery days. As discussed in Section 2.6, by normalising, a more consistent definition of the data is obtained, usually resulting in better models. The analysis was carried out both for 'orders received' and 'invoiced sales'. The analysis shown here relates to 'orders received' but, insofar as the influence of promotional effects are concerned, the models are not dissimilar to those obtained using 'invoiced sales'. Since promotional effects were difficult to quantify, the promotional series were represented by intervention variables which took the value '1' when a promotion took place and a value '0' when no promotion activity took place.

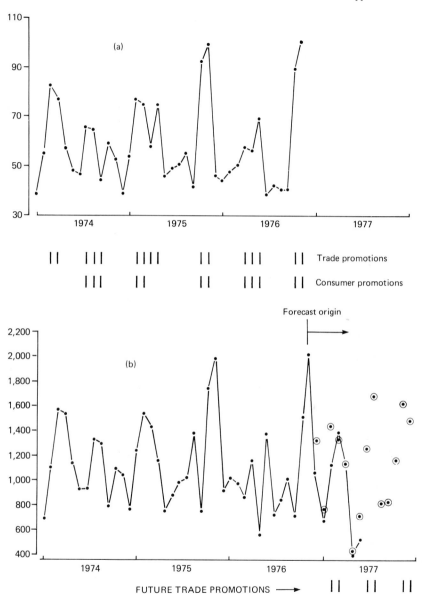

Fig 31. (a) Sales data, normalised by dividing by number of selling days, and associated trade and consumer promotions; (b) Original (unnormalised) data, together with forecasts from origin 1976, period 12 at lead times 1, 2, ... , 14 using intervention model (g) and known future dates of trade promotions. Also, shown are 7 future values of sales when they came to hand.

Initially, trade promotions were classified into 'strong', 'medium' and 'weak' categories according to an assessment made by the organisation's Marketing Department. It was found that 'strong' and 'medium' promotions had very similar effects whereas 'weak' promotions had no discernible effect on sales. Accordingly, in the subsequent analysis, 'strong' and 'medium' trade promotions were classified together, and called 'trade promotions', while 'weak' promotions were ignored.

The first 5 rows in Table 11 show respectively,

(a) the univariate model fitted to the normalised sales series, ignoring the effect of promotions,

(b) an intervention model relating sales to trade promotions, whether 'strong' or 'medium',

(c) an intervention model relating sales to 'strong' trade and 'medium' trade promotions,

(d) an intervention model relating sales to consumer promotions,

(e) an intervention model relating sales to consumer and trade promotions.

It is not possible to use prewhitening to identify intervention models (see Appendix A.4). Thus, to illustrate how these models were fitted, suppose $Y_t$ is the normalised sales series and $\xi_t$ is a variable representing the occurrence of a particular type of promotion. It was believed by some in the organisation that the effect of a promotion this month is to increase sales in that same month. Thus, the model may be written

$$Y_t = \omega_0 \xi_t + N_t \tag{17}$$

where $N_t$ is a noise or error, representing that part of the sales series that can not be explained by trade promotions. However, others believed that a promotion this month affected not only sales this month but also sales the following month. In this case the model

$$Y_t = (\omega_0 - \omega_1 B)\xi_t + N_t \tag{18}$$

could be entertained. As in previous examples, the univariate model for $Y_t$ given in the first row of Table 11 can be used as an initial guess of the structure of the noise, that is

$$\nabla N_t = (1 - \theta_1 B - \theta_2 B^2)(1 - \Theta_1 B^{13} - \Theta_2 B^{26})a_t. \tag{19}$$

Combining (19) with, for example (18), models of the form

$$\nabla Y_t = (\omega_0 - \omega_1 B)\nabla \xi_t + (1 - \theta_1 B - \theta_2 B^2)(1 - \Theta_1 B^{13} - \Theta_2 B^{26})a_t \tag{20}$$

**Table 11**
Summary of models fitted to sales data (orders received) normalized by dividing by the number of delivery days per accounting period ($N$ = 38 data points).

| Model | Intervention Variables | Estimated model | Residual standard deviation | Largest residuals |
|---|---|---|---|---|
| (a) | None: univariate model only | $\nabla Y_t = (1 - 0.45B - 0.48B^2)(1 + 0.40B^{13} + 0.52B^{26})a_{1t}$<br>±0.15  ±0.15  ±0.15  ±0.10 | 1439 | $a_{24} = 2.4\sigma$ |
| (b) | $\xi_{1t} = \begin{cases}1, & \text{Trade Promotion}\\0, & \text{otherwise}\end{cases}$<br>$\xi_{2t} = \begin{cases}1, & \text{strong trade promotion}\\0, & \text{otherwise}\end{cases}$ | $\nabla Y_t = 2387\nabla\xi_{1t} + (1 - 0.53B - 0.38B^2)(1 + 0.55B^{13})a_{2t}$<br>±382   ±0.16  ±0.16   ±0.20 | 1090 | $a_{10} = -2.0\sigma$<br>$a_{11} = 2.4\sigma$ |
| (c) | $\xi_{3t} = \begin{cases}1, & \text{medium trade promotion}\\0, & \text{otherwise}\end{cases}$ | $\nabla Y_t = 2213\nabla\xi_{2t} + 2619\nabla\xi_{3t} + (1 - 0.54B - 0.37B^2)(1 + 0.57B^{13})a_{3t}$<br>±462  ±594  ±0.17  ±0.17   ±0.21 | 1101 | $a_{10} = -1.9\sigma$<br>$a_{11} = 2.3\sigma$ |
| (d) | $\xi_{4t} = \begin{cases}1, & \text{consumer promotion}\\0, & \text{otherwise}\end{cases}$ | $\nabla Y_t = 2184\nabla\xi_{4t} + (1 - 0.38B - 0.51B^2)(1 + 0.35B^{13})a_{4t}$<br>±528   ±0.15  ±0.15   ±0.21 | 1353 | $a_3 = 2.5\sigma$<br>$a_{10} = -1.7\sigma$<br>$a_{11} = 2.0\sigma$ |
| (e) | $\xi_{1t} = \begin{cases}1,\\0,\end{cases}$ trade promotion<br>$\xi_{4t} = \begin{cases}1,\\0,\end{cases}$ consumer promotion | $\nabla Y_t = 2778\nabla\xi_{1t} - 572\nabla\xi_{4t} + (1 - 0.56B - 0.35B^2)(1 + 0.61B^{13})a_{5t}$<br>±615  ±638  ±0.17   ±0.17    ±0.20 | 1095 | $a_{10} = -2.0\sigma$<br>$a_{11} = 2.3\sigma$ |
| (f) | $\xi_{5t} = \begin{cases}1,\\0,\end{cases}$ trade *and* consumer promotion<br>$\xi_{6t} = \begin{cases}1,\\0,\end{cases}$ trade promotion only | $\nabla Y_t = 2206\nabla\xi_{5t} + 2778\nabla\xi_{6t} + (1 - 0.56B - 0.35B^2)(1 + 0.61B^{13})a_{6t}$<br>±403  ±615  ±0.17   ±0.17    ±0.20 | 1095 | $a_{10} = -1.9\sigma$<br>$a_{11} = 2.3\sigma$ |
| (g) | $\xi_{1t} = \begin{cases}1,\\0,\end{cases}$ trade promotion<br>$\xi_{7t} = \begin{cases}1, & \text{year 3, period 4 (2 sales forces)}\\0, & \text{otherwise}\end{cases}$ | $\nabla Y_t = 2012\nabla\xi_{1t} - 1607\nabla\xi_{7,t-1} + (1 - 0.51B - 0.46B^2)(1 + 0.57B^{13})a_{7t}$<br>±353  ±949   ±0.17  ±0.17   ±0.21 | 1045 | $a_{10} = -1.9\sigma$<br>$a_{11} = 2.3\sigma$ |

were entertained and then fitted for different categories of promotional variable $\xi_t$. Then parameters were omitted if they turned out to be small compared with their standard errors and the simpler models refitted. In this way conflicting views as to the effect of certain promotions could be resolved.

The following comments may be made concerning the final models which are shown in Table 11:

(i) The univariate model (a) displays strong seasonality, most of it due to the strongly seasonal nature of the promotional activity.

(ii) Model (b) shows that trade promotions have a strong effect on sales, the estimate $\hat{\omega}_0 = 2387$ being over six times its standard error. Note that the seasonal part of the model has simplified considerably as a result of introducing the promotional effect. Note also that the large residual at 1974, period 11 ($t = 24$) in the univariate model (a) has now disappeared since it has been explained by the promotion variable at that point.

(iii) Model (c) shows that if promotions are split into 'strong' promotions and 'medium' promotions, these two types of promotion have effects on sales that are similar in magnitude. Moreover, since model (c) does not result in a better fit than model (b), there is no advantage in distinguishing between 'strong' and 'medium' trade promotions, as mentioned above.

(iv) Model (d) suggests that consumer promotions also affect sales but that the effect is weaker since the residual variance is much larger for model (d) than for model (b).

(v) Model (e) shows the effect of introducing trade and consumer promotions simultaneously. It indicates that consumer promotions have no effect, seeming to negate the result implied by Model (d). However, closer examination of the promotion series reveals that whereas trade promotions are sometimes held in the absence of consumer promotions, consumer promotions are always held at the same time as trade promotions – that is, there are no times when consumer promotions are held on their own. Hence, it is difficult to disentangle the two effects. Thus, the strong effect due to consumer promotions in Model (d) could be due to the fact that trade promotions were held simultaneously.

(vi) To clarify the position, Model (f) was fitted using two other intervention variables defined as follows:

$$\xi_{5t} = \begin{cases} 1, & \text{trade and consumer promotions occur simultaneously,} \\ 0, & \text{otherwise,} \end{cases}$$

$$\xi_{6t} = \begin{cases} 1, & \text{trade promotions occur on their own,} \\ 0, & \text{otherwise.} \end{cases}$$

Model (f) shows that it makes no difference to the magnitude of the trade promotion effect if it occurs with or without consumer promotions – again suggesting that consumer promotions have no effect and confirming the results implied by Model (e).

This example raises interesting questions as to how promotional activity should be carried out most effectively. It suggests that organisations should not only undertake promotional activity but also, at the same time, should take more care to generate the right kind of information in order to determine the effectiveness of their promotional activity. In this example, this could have been achieved if some periods had trade promotions on their own, some periods had consumer promotions on their own and some periods had neither trade nor consumer promotions. If this had been done it would have been possible to separate out the effects of trade and consumer promotions with greater precision.

(vii) Models (b) to (f) have negative residuals from 1976, Period 5 to 1976, Period 9. Since this was unusual behaviour, the organisation were asked what happened at this point in time. It transpired that 1976, Period 4 corresponded to the splitting of the sales force into two separate sales forces. The reorganisation resulting from this change resulted in a temporary loss in sales for a few months. In Model (g) the introduction of the two sales forces is represented by adding a further intervention variable into Model (b), the best model obtained previously. It is seen that the introduction of the two sales forces has a significant negative effect on sales in the period after its introduction. Model (g) shows that the inclusion of just two variables, namely the occurrence of trade promotions and the introduction of the two sales forces, has resulted in a very big reduction in residual standard deviation, as compared with the univariate model (a).

Figure 31(b) shows forecasts of the renormalised sales (that is the forecasts of the normalised sales multiplied by the number of delivery days per accounting period) based on model (g), using data up to a time origin 1976, period 12 and future knowledge that promotions would be held in certain periods. Also shown are the actual sales during the first seven of these months, when they came to hand.

## 3.4. *An application of multivariate stochastic models to the sales of competitive products*

This analysis was part of a wider study of competition between several products in the European market. Figure 32 shows a plot of the logarithms of quarterly sales data for two such products, which are designated Product 1 and

Product 2. The data had been previously seasonally adjusted using a standard package, against the advice of the writer. Some consequences of this act are described later.

Figure 32 shows that both products are characterised by sustained growth which is approximately linear in the logarithms and hence exponential for the original series. The range-mean plots (not shown) for the two products revealed that there was a well defined linear dependence between the range and mean for both series, suggesting that a logarithmic transformation would be appropriate in each case. (See Appendix A.1 for a further discussion of data transformations). In this example a logarithmic transformation not only ensures that the scatter of the transformed variables is independent of the level, but also converts the approximately exponential growth into approximately linear growth.

There was prior evidence that a transfer function model, (implying a unidirectional relationship between the two series) would not be appropriate in this case since it was known that sales of Product 1 affected sales of Product 2 and vice versa. Hence, it was assumed initially that a multivariate stochastic model would be more appropriate than a transfer function model to describe this situation. If such an assumption turned out to be incorrect, then the model building process should reveal that a transfer function is more appropriate, in which case a transfer function model could then be fitted.

The first step in a multivariate stochastic analysis is to build univariate models for each time series separately (another illustration of 'learning to grovel' before attempting to walk' as emphasised in Section 2.6). Denoting the time series for sales of Product 1 by $z_{1t}$ and the sales of Product 2 by $z_{2t}$, the usual identification, estimation and checking stages for univariate models (see Box and Jenkins, 1970) led to the following univariate models fitted separately to each series:

$$\nabla \ln z_{1t} = 0.056 + \alpha_{1t} \qquad (21)$$
$$\pm 0.010$$

where $\alpha_{1t}$ is a random series with variance $\sigma_1^2 = 0.002991$ (per cent standard deviation = 5.5%) and

$$\nabla \ln z_{2t} = 0.042 + (1 - 0.70B)\alpha_{2t} \qquad (22)$$
$$\pm 0.002 \qquad \pm 0.11$$

where $\alpha_{2t}$ is a random series with variance $\sigma_2^2 = 0.002044$ (per cent standard deviation = 4.5%).

Figure 33 shows the prewhitened cross correlation function between the two series, that is the cross correlation function between $\alpha_{1t}$ and $\alpha_{2t}$ at positive and

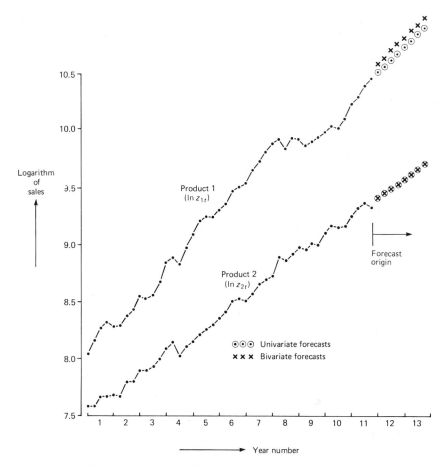

Fig 32. Sales of two competitive products, together with forecasts for lead times 1, 2, . . . , 8 from origin $t = 44$; quarterly observations for 11 years.

negative lags. The two correlations which stand out above the two standard error limits are at lags $k = -1$ and $+1$. The positive correlation at lag $k = +1$ implies that there is a tendency for an increase in the sales of Product 1 this quarter to be accompanied by an increase in sales of Product 2 in the next quarter. The negative correlation at lag $k = -1$ implies that there is a tendency for an increase in sales of Product 2 this quarter to be accompanied by a decrease in sales of Product 1 in the next quarter. This result stems from the fact that Product 2 can genuinely be substituted for Product 1 but not vice versa — the end use for Product 1 requires that Product 2 be also used.

Based on the cross correlation function of Figure 33, a model

$$\alpha_{1t} = a_{1t} - \theta_{12}a_{2,t-1}$$
$$\alpha_{2t} = -\theta_{21}a_{1,t-1} + a_{2t} \tag{23}$$

was postulated for the residuals from the fitted univariate models. On eliminating $\alpha_{1t}$ and $\alpha_{2t}$ between (21), (22) and (23), we can tentatively entertain the following structure

$$\nabla ln\, z_{1t} = c_1 + a_{1t} - \theta_{12,1}Ba_{2t},$$

$$\nabla \ln z_{2t} = c_2 - (\theta_{21,1}B + \theta_{21,2}B^2)a_{1t} + (1 - \theta_{22,1}B)a_{2t}$$

for the bivariate stochastic model describing $z_{1t}$ and $z_{2t}$ where, for example, $\theta_{21,1} = -\theta\theta_{21}$. The final model, after three iterations of identification, fitting and checking, was

$$\nabla \ln z_{1t} = 0.058 + (1 + 0.42B)a_{1t} - 0.84Ba_{2t},$$
$$\pm 0.005 \qquad \pm 0.15 \qquad \pm 0.17$$

$$\nabla \ln z_{2t} = 0.042 + (0.28B - 0.24B^2)a_{1t} + (1 - 0.75B)a_{2t} \tag{24}$$
$$\pm 0.001 \quad \pm 0.13 \quad \pm 0.11 \qquad \qquad \pm 0.11$$

with residual variance $\sigma_1^2 = 0.002039$ (per cent standard deviation = 4.5%) for Product 1 and residual variance $\sigma_2^2 = 0.001750$ (per cent standard deviation = 4.2%) for Product 2. With models of this kind there is a further

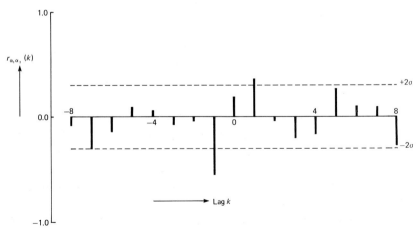

Fig 33. Prewhitened cross correlation function between sales of two competitive products.

Table 12a
Per cent standard deviations of forecast errors at different lead times corresponding
to different models fitted to products 1 and 2

| Lead Time | Per cent standard deviation | | | |
|---|---|---|---|---|
| | Product 1 | | Product 2 | |
| | Univariate model | Bivariate model | Univariate model | Bivariate model |
| 1 | 5.47 | 4.52 | 4.52 | 4.18 |
| 2 | 8.59 | 7.88 | 4.72 | 4.56 |
| 3 | 10.84 | 10.19 | 4.90 | 4.69 |
| 4 | 12.70 | 12.06 | 5.08 | 4.82 |
| 5 | 14.32 | 13.68 | 5.25 | 4.95 |
| 6 | 15.78 | 15.13 | 5.42 | 5.07 |
| 7 | 17.11 | 16.45 | 5.58 | 5.18 |
| 8 | 18.34 | 17.67 | 5.74 | 5.30 |

Table 12b
Forecasts of Products 1 and 2 for lead times 1, 2, . . . , 8 quarters from origin
44 based on (a) separate univariate models for each product, (b) a bivariate model.

| Observation number | Product 1 | | Product 2 | |
|---|---|---|---|---|
| | Univariate model forecasts | Bivariate model forecasts | Univariate model forecasts | Bivariate model forecasts |
| 45 | 36,959 | 39,785 | 12,322 | 12,349 |
| 46 | 39,108 | 42,177 | 12,856 | 12,873 |
| 47 | 41,382 | 44,713 | 13,412 | 13,431 |
| 48 | 43,788 | 47,401 | 13,993 | 14,014 |
| 49 | 46,334 | 50,251 | 14,599 | 14,622 |
| 50 | 49,028 | 53,272 | 15,231 | 15,256 |
| 51 | 51,879 | 56,474 | 15,891 | 15,917 |
| 52 | 54,895 | 59,869 | 16,579 | 16,608 |

parameter to be considered, namely the correlation between the residuals $a_{1t}$
and $a_{2t}$ at simultaneous times, which was 0.24 in this example. Alternatively,
this value can be interpreted as the correlation between the one-step-ahead
forecast errors when the model is used in a forecasting mode.

Table 12a compares the forecasting performance of the univariate and bivariate models at various lead times.

Table 12b and Figure 32 show forecasts made 8 quarters ahead from origin
$t = 44$ using the univariate and bivariate models. From this origin, the univariate

forecasts are close to the bivariate forecasts but this will not be true in general.

This model was useful in explaining the substitution effects between these two competitive products but from a practical point of view was not entirely satisfactory for two reasons:

(i) The constants in the fitted bivariate model (24) above have a readily understandable physical significance in that they represent the quarterly growth rates of sales. For example, the constant 0.058 in the Product 1 model represents a 5.8% average quarterly growth rate for that product. Because of the stability of this market over the period analysed, the growth rate had been approximately constant. Unfortunately, the model (24) would constrain the forecasts to grow at this rate *indefinitely*. If, as seems likely, it were felt that the growth rate might change in the future then, to generate forecasts, values for the constants could be used which are different from those obtained from the historical data analysed. This is not entirely satisfactory and a better approach would be to try and remove the constant by introducing an explanatory variable into the model to explain the growth of the series. However, independently of whether it is possible to find such an explanatory variable, it is better to use data which has not been seasonally adjusted. If the latter approach had been used in this example, differencing of the form $\nabla\nabla_4$ would have been needed and the constants would have been eliminated. Thus, the model would be able to adapt more readily to changes in growth rate.

(ii) The residual cross correlations (see Figure 34) of Model (24) have peaks

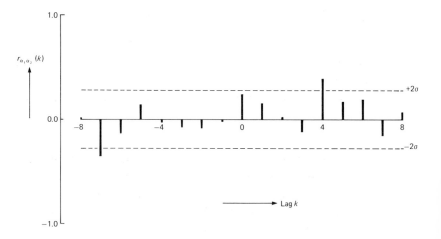

Fig 34. Residual cross correlation function corresponding to bivariate stochastic model fitted to sales of two competitive products.

in the neighbourhood of lags 4 and 8, corresponding to residual seasonality due to inadequate seasonal adjustment. The residual autocorrelations (not shown in Figure 34) also display similar behaviour. It was decided not to complicate the models quoted here to allow for this residual seasonal behaviour. However, it will affect the forecasting performance of the model.

Thus, there are two reasons why the original seasonal data would have been more suitable for model building than the seasonally adjusted data. Subsequently, a model was fitted to the original unadjusted data. This model was more complicated than the one quoted here and had only a marginal superiority over the length of record for which the model was fitted. However, at a later time period when the rate of growth slackened, its forecasting performance was markedly better than the model based on a fixed growth rate.

### 3.5. An application of multivariate transfer function models to sales volume – price relationships

This analysis formed part of a major project to investigate the effect of alternative pricing policies on the sales of a particular group of consumer products. The market situation was characterised by sensitivity to price and a high degree of competition due to a variety of factors.

The data to be used for illustration has already been shown in Figure 12 but is shown again in Figure 35 in a slightly different form. Figure 35 shows plots of:

$Y_{1t}$ : the monthly sales of a group of products, designated Group 1, sold by the organisation who commissioned the study,

$Y_{2t}$ : the corresponding monthly sales of a group of competitive products, designated Group 2, and sold by organisations other than the one which commissioned the study,

$P_{1t}$ : the proportional changes in a volume weighted price index for Group 1,

$P_{2t}$ : the proportional changes in a corresponding volume weighted price index for Group 2.

Economic theories abound as to the expected relationships between consumption and price. In business forecasting, at least, any correspondence between such theory and the real world seems to be governed more by a 'cosmic random number generator' than by any other cause. Such price-volume relationships are usually *non-linear* in the sense that if a change of $\delta P$ in price eventually produces a change of $\delta Y$ in consumption, then a change of $2\delta P$ in price will not necessarily produce a change of $2\delta Y$ in consumption. One way to deal with such non-linearities is to use 'theory' to suggest some form of non-linear relationship. The approach adopted here was to use empirical investigation to explore the nature of the non-linearity. It will be shown that there was evidence not only of non-linear effects but also of fundamentally different mechanisms at work for small and large price changes. Such conclusions are not untypical in the writer's experience.

*Single output models.* The first step in developing a multiple output–multiple input model (see Appendix A.6) is to build single output models separately for each output – in this example this involves building separate models relating:
– Sales of Product 1 to Price of Product 1 and Price of Product 2,
– Sales of Product 2 to Price of Product 1 and Price of Product 2.
Thus, we are faced initially with the problem of building two separate one output–two input models. Early on in the study, it was found that the price of Product 2 had no direct effect on the sales of Product 1 and the price of Product 1 no direct effect on the sales of Product 2. Accordingly, the outcomes of this initial analysis were two separate single output–single input models relating the Sales Volume and Price of each product.

In the early explorations, the effects of individual price changes were investigated. Instead of working with the price variable itself, as in Figure 12, the proportional change in price was used as in Figure 35. Thus, the price series are represented as a series of 'pulses', with heights equal to the proportional changes, at the points in time at which those changes took place. The rationale behind this definition of the price variables is given below.

Two conclusions emerged from this exploratory analysis:

(1) small price changes had a 'local effect' in the sense that they temporarily depressed sales for one or two months but did not have a lasting effect,

(2) large price changes, in contrast, produced a relatively large drop in sales in the first one or two months but thereafter produced a *permanent* drop in the level of sales.

Thus, for practical purposes, price increases could be classified into two categories called 'small' and 'large', depending on whether they resulted in a mechanism of the form (1) or (2) above.

The first two rows of Table 13 show the final models arrived at after a few iterations of identification, fitting and checking of these models. In Table 13 the price variable $P_{1t}$ has been separated into two variables:

$X_{1t}$ : proportional price changes for Product 1 less than or equal to 0.20 (20%),

$X_{2t}$ : proportional price changes for Product 1 greater than 0.20 (20%).

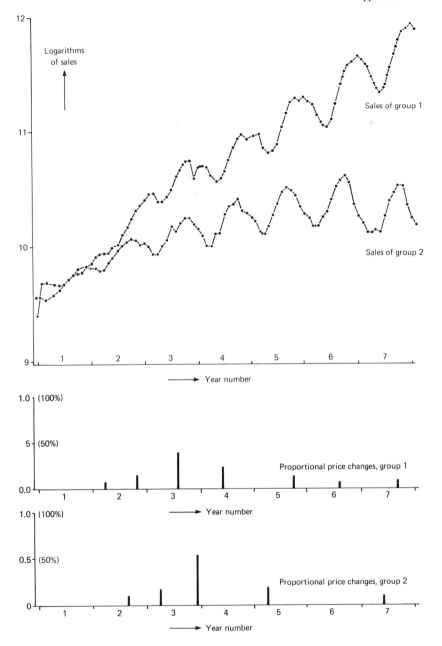

Fig 35. Sales of two groups of intermediate products, together with corresponding proportional changes in deflated price indices: monthly data for a period of seven years.

Similarly, the price variable $P_{2t}$ has been separated into two variables:

$X_{3t}$ : proportional price changes for Product 2 less than or equal to 0.20 (20%),

$X_{4t}$ : proportional price changes for Product 2 greater than 0.20 (20%).

Preliminary analysis showed that the sales volume series needed logarithmic transformation. Bearing in mind that expressing a price as a proportional change is a similar operation to taking logarithms, we see that the proposed relationships essentially relate the logarithm of sales to the logarithm of price, the conventional way for representing consumption-price relationships in economics.

The structure of the first single input model in Table 13, relating the sales of product Group 1 to the weighted price index of that group, is better understood if the model is written in the form

$$\ln Y_{1t} = \underset{\pm 0.074\ \ \pm 0.074}{-(0.204 + 0.096B)X_{1t}} - \frac{\overset{\pm 0.052\ \ \pm 0.052}{(0.250 - 0.119B)}}{1 - B} X_{2t} + N_{1t} \tag{25}$$

where the noise model is given by

$$\nabla\nabla_{12} N_{1t} = \alpha_{1t} \tag{26}$$

and $\alpha_{1t}$ is a random series with variance $\sigma_1^2 = 0.001149$.

Combining (25) and (26), we obtain the transfer function-noise model given in the first row of Table 13. The interpretation of (25) is as follows:

(1) A 1% change among the class of 'small' price changes depresses sales by 0.2% in the first month and approximately 0.1% in the second month, that is 0.3% over the two months (to preserve the confidentiality of the data, it has been scaled and so the actual parameter estimates quoted here are not the same as those for the unscaled data).

(2) The relationship between sales volume $\ln Y_{1t}$ and a 'large' price change $X_{2t}$ may be written

$$\ln Y_{1t} = -\frac{(0.250 - 0.119B)}{1 - B} X_{2t}$$

$$= -0.250 X_{2t} - 0.131 (X_{2,t-1} + X_{2,t-2} + \ldots) \tag{27}$$

Table 13
Summary of single output and multiple output transfer function-noise models fitted to sales volume and price series, relating to two groups of competitive products. *Key.* $X_{1t}$: price changes less than or equal to 20% for Group 1; $X_{2t}$: price changes greater than 20% for Group 1; $X_{3t}$: price changes less than or equal to 20% for Group 2; $X_{4t}$: price changes greater than 20% for Group 2

| Model type | Estimated model | Residual variance | Per cent standard deviation |
|---|---|---|---|
| Sales of group 1 ($Y_{1t}$) versus price of group 1 ($X_{1t}, X_{2t}$) (1 output–2 input) | $\nabla\nabla_{12} \ln Y_{1t} = -(0.204 + 0.096B)\,\nabla\nabla_{12} X_{1t} - (0.250 - 0.119B)\nabla_{12}X_{2t} + \alpha_{1t}$ <br> $\phantom{xxxxxxxxxx}\pm0.074\ \pm0.074\phantom{xxxxxxxx}\pm0.052\ \pm0.052$ | 0.001149 | 3.39 |
| Sales of group 2 ($Y_{2t}$) versus price of group 2 ($X_{3t}, X_{4t}$) (1 output–2 input) | $\nabla\nabla_{12} \ln Y_{2t} = -(0.209 + 0.049B)\,\nabla\nabla_{12} X_{3t} - (0.245 - 0.112B)\,\nabla_{12}X_{4t} + \dfrac{1}{(1-0.66B)}\alpha_{2t}$ <br> $\phantom{xxxxxxxxxx}\pm0.031\ \pm0.031\phantom{xxxxxxx}\pm0.022\ \pm0.022\phantom{xxxxxxxxxx}\pm0.09$ | 0.0003809 | 1.95 |
| Sales of group 1 and sales of group 2 versus price of group 1 and price of group 2 (2 outputs–4 inputs) | $\nabla\nabla_{12} \ln Y_t = -(0.236 + 0.051B)\,\nabla\nabla_{12}X_{1t} - (0.220 - 0.166B)\nabla_{12}X_{2t} + N_{1t}$ <br> $\phantom{xxxxxxx}\pm0.070\ \pm0.072\phantom{xxxxxxx}\pm0.043\ \pm0.042$ <br> $\nabla\nabla_{12} \ln Y_{2t} = -(0.230 + 0.059B)\nabla\nabla_{12}X_{3t} - (0.278 - 0.098B)\nabla_{12} X_{4t} + N_{2t}$ <br> $\phantom{xxxxxxx}\pm0.027\ \pm0.026\phantom{xxxxxxx}\pm0.018\ \pm0.018$ <br><br> $\begin{bmatrix} 1 & 0.36B \\ & \pm0.19 \\ -0.33B & 1-0.50B \\ \pm0.06 & \pm0.11 \end{bmatrix}\begin{bmatrix} N_{1t} \\ N_{2t} \end{bmatrix} = \begin{bmatrix} a_{1t} \\ a_{2t} \end{bmatrix}$ | $\sigma_1^2 = 0.001116$ <br><br> $\sigma_2^2 = 0.000250$ | 3.34 <br><br> 1.58 |

Thus, for a 'large' price change, a 1% price increase this month decreases sales in this month by approximately 0.25% and then produces a permanent drop of 0.13% in each month thereafter.

As emphasised in several other places such a model must obviously be 'wrong' since all models are wrong. However, what is claimed is that it provides an adequate representation of this data and that extensive checking of the model failed to reveal any need for elaboration.

*Two output–four input model.* As indicated above, the two groups of products being discussed here were sold in a highly competitive market. In this sense it was a little surprising to discover, for example, that the price of Product 2 does not seem to have an influence on the sales volume of Product 1, since price is known to be an important factor influencing the decision to purchase the product. However, it would appear that, in this example, there is a further interaction between the sales of the two product groups, which is not only price dependent but also supply and quality dependent.

The nature of this interaction may be studied by taking the residuals $\alpha_{1t}$ and $\alpha_{2t}$ from the single output models given in rows 1 and 2 of Table 13 and calculating their cross correlation function at different lags. Figure 36 shows this 'prewhitened' cross correlation function which has moderately large correlations for both positive and negative lags. This implies two way feedback between the sales of the two products, after allowing for the effect of price. On the basis of the cross correlation function of Figure 36 there is a marginal preference for an autoregressive hypothesis, due to the presence of damped sine wave behaviour on both sides of zero lag. Thus, as a first step, the multivariate stochastic model

$$\begin{bmatrix} 1 & -\phi_{12}B \\ -\phi_{21}B & 1 \end{bmatrix} \begin{bmatrix} \alpha_{1t} \\ \alpha_{2t} \end{bmatrix} = \begin{bmatrix} a_{1t} \\ a_{2t} \end{bmatrix} \tag{28}$$

was postulated for the residuals $\alpha_{1t}$ and $\alpha_{2t}$ of the single output models. On combining (28) with the two single output models given in rows 1 and 2 of Table 13, we are led to postulate a multiple output–multiple input model

$$\nabla\nabla_{12} \ln Y_{1t} = (\omega_{0,11} - \omega_{1,11}B)\nabla\nabla_{12}X_{1t} + (\omega_{0,12} - \omega_{1,12}B)\nabla_{12}X_{2t} + N_{1t},$$

$$\nabla\nabla_{12} \ln Y_{2t} = (\omega_{0,23} - \omega_{1,23}B)\nabla\nabla_{12}X_{3t} + (\omega_{0,24} - \omega_{1,24}B)\nabla_{12}X_{4t} + N_{2t}$$

where the noise model is given by

$$\begin{bmatrix} 1 & -\phi_{12,1}B - \phi_{12,2}B^2 \\ -\phi_{21,1}B & 1 - \phi_{22,1}B \end{bmatrix} \begin{bmatrix} N_{1t} \\ N_{2t} \end{bmatrix} = \begin{bmatrix} a_{1t} \\ a_{2t} \end{bmatrix} \tag{29}$$

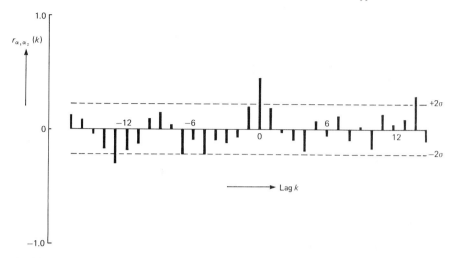

Fig 36. Prewhitened cross correlation function based on the residuals $\alpha_{1t}$ and $\alpha_{2t}$ from the single output transfer function models (Table 13) fitted to Sales data for two competitive products (plotted in Figure 35).

The final model, after four iterations of identification, fitting and checking (See Appendix A.6) is shown in the third row of Table 13.

The volume-price relationships obtained from the single output models are not substantially altered in moving from the single input models to the more complex multiple output–multiple input model. However, the improved noise structure has resulted in smaller residual variances and smaller standard errors for the parameter estimates.

The model based on the unscaled data (as distinct from the scaled data used for analysis here) provided considerable insight into the functioning of this market. In particular, it enabled the effect of price to be separated from other competitive factors such as quality and service, as determined by the availability of supply. The model was used to simulate alternative pricing policies and resulted in some changes in future pricing policy.

# Part 4 Comparisons with econometric modelling

Reference is made at various points in the preceeding sections to certain differences between the approach to building time series models described in this publication and econometric model building. It is appropriate here to bring together and amplify these comments. The present discussion expands on some remarks made elsewhere (Jenkins, 1977).

## 4.1. Seasonality

Classical thinking in economics focusses attention on a decomposition of a time series into a 'seasonal component', 'trend' and 'residual series'. It is conventional in econometric model building to remove the seasonality in a series by some method of seasonal adjustment, for example the Shiskin X-11 method. As indicated in several places, such seasonal adjustment methods are:

(a) *arbitrary*, since there is no unique way of effecting such a decomposition,

(b) *inflexible*, since they apply virtually the same method of adjustment to all series, irrespective of their statistical properties,

(c) *harmful* in their effect on the adjusted series, since some of the 'trend' and 'residual series' is removed as well; conversely, not all the seasonality is removed, leaving behind correlations at multiples of the seasonal period, as observed in Section 3.4.,

(d) *confusing*, since the original data is lost sight of,

(e) *inefficient*, in the sense that forecasts obtained by adding the forecasts for the seasonal and non-seasonal parts of the series can be inaccurate.

In contrast, the approach described in previous sections:

(1) describes the 'seasonality', 'trend' and 'residual series' under the umbrella of *one overall model*,

(2) allows for many different types of *adaption* with time in the seasonal pattern.

This does not mean that seasonal adjustment is not helpful. On the contrary, when a model has been built it can be used to separate both *series and forecasts* into components, thereby helping in the interpretation of the forecasts.

## 4.2. Trends

It is conventional in econometric model building to use polynomials and dummy variables to describe 'trends'. Such methods are unsatisfactory since:

(a) it is unlikely that such *deterministic* trends are adequate to describe the development of observed time series, implying as they do that growth rates remain constant indefinitely,

(b) the introduction of dummy variables to describe changes in trends at specific points implies prior knowledge of some structural change; it also implies that the trend mechanism continues to be deterministic after the *assumed* structural change.

In contrast, the approach advocated here accounts for non-seasonal and seasonal 'trends' by introducing differencing terms into the model, thereby ensuring that the trends are *stochastic* or *adaptive* and not deterministic.

## 4.3. Lag structures

It is conventional in control theory (and the mathematics for doing so has been around for over 100 years) to describe linear dynamic effects by means of what are called *rational lag structures*, or in the terminology of previous sections, by autoregressive – moving average models (see Box and Jenkins, 1961, 1963, 1965; Aström, 1966, 1970). In econometrics there has been a tendency to give these lag structures (which have been known to mathematicians, physicists and control engineers for a very long time) names in very special cases – for example 'distributed lags' or 'Koyck lags'. The introduction of general rational lags in econometrics seems to date from Jorgensen (1966) and Dhrymes (1970) but their use is far from being widespread. Instead, models use regression coefficients at each lag, resulting in over parameterisation and estimates with poor statistical properties.

In contrast, the prewhitening techniques described in previous sections result in parsimonious lag structures whose parameters can be well estimated.

## 4.4. 'Error' or 'noise' structures

Even if rational lags are used, there is no guarantee that effective models will result since error, or noise, structures can have a major effect on the estimation of the lag structure. A typical misconception in econometrics is exemplified by the following simple model relating an output $Y_t$ to an input $X_t$:

$$Y_t = aY_{t-1} + cX_t + e_t \tag{30}$$

Introducing the backward shift operator $B$, the model (30) may be written as

$$Y_t = \frac{c}{1 - aB} X_t + \frac{1}{1 - aB} e_t$$

Thus, a consequence of the formulation (30) is that, independently of the structure of $e_t$, there is a common factor $(1 - aB)$ in the transfer function and the noise. This is unrealistic and also creates problems in estimating the model parameters. Concentration on model structures such as (30) seems to have been influenced by a desire to write models in a form which enables linear least squares (or multi-stage least squares) to be applied. Thus, preoccupation with regression analysis and linear least squares has often diverted attention from better specifications of lag and error structures in econometrics.

There has also been a reluctance to use moving average structures as well as autoregressive structures in the error. As remarked earlier, failure to incorporate moving average as well as autoregressive structures can sometimes lead to a model with too many parameters, violating the principle of parsimony.

In contrast, the noise structures incorporated in the transfer function models of Appendix A.3 include non-seasonal and seasonal differencing to induce station-arity in the errors, as well as non-seasonal and seasonal autoregressive and moving average structures.

## 4.5. Model building

The most serious weakness in econometric model building seems to be the absence of a model building *methodology*. It is argued by many that 'economic theory' should be the sole arbiter as to what structures should be built into a model. In the same way that a knowledge of engineering science, or biology, or marketing, is essential for the application of model building techniques in these areas, model building in an economic environment must clearly be approached with an appreciation of what theory and prior knowledge has to say about a particular problem situation. However, no 'theory' in any subject is sacrosant. At a time when economic theory is finding it difficult to explain steady-state relationships, let alone dynamic effects, there is little justification for dogmatic assertion that 'economic theory' should be the only factor to be taken into account. Again, there is often genuine doubt in theory as to whether a variable $X$ affects $Y$, or $Y$ affects $X$, or whether there is two way feedback between the two variables. In such circumstances a more sensible approach would seem to be to use theory and prior knowledge to influence the choice of variables for a particular situation and then to combine this knowledge with empirical investigation in order to arrive at models which are representationally adequate. Thus, many models which claim to make economic 'sense' turn out to make statistical 'nonsense' due to a variety of reasons discussed in Sections 4.1–4.6. A desirable objective is that a model should be sensible both from the point of view of economics and statistics.

*Identification.* Because of the absence of adequate identification techniques, such as *prewhitening*, there is a tendency in econometrics for many *spurious explanatory variables* to be introduced into a model. The use of inadequate error structures then reinforces the belief that some variables are important when they are not. It should be borne in mind that when fitting, for example, a single output–single input transfer function we are essentially concerned with answering two questions:

(1) What weights must be applied to current and past values of the input $X_t$ to forecast the output $Y_t$?

(2) What weights must be applied to past values of the $Y_t$ series to forecast $Y_t$?

With an inadequate error structure, the weights are automatically transferred to current and past values of the $X_t$ series. In contrast, correct formulation and estimation of the error structure may lead to the conclusion that most of the weight should be applied to the past history of the $Y_t$ series and that inclusion of the $X$-variables provides no further useful explanatory information. As such, the occurrence of very high $R^2$ (square of the multiple correlation coefficient) values in many econometric relationships has more to do with incorrect error specification than with the 'strength of the relationship' between the $Y_t$ and $X_t$ variables.

*Large models.* The problem of spurious variables and regression coefficients in econometrics is exacerbated by a puzzling tendency to regard *size* and *complexity* as desirable characteristics of a model. The 'track record' of such large models, in terms of their forecasting performance, is not very encouraging and the reasons for this indifferent performance are not difficult to find, namely:

(a) if prior economic considerations are allowed to exert a dominant influence on model structures, then it is inevitable that too many variables and too many parameters will be included. (This problem is not unique to econometrics and occurs in many branches of science.)

(b) Given such complex model structures, it is inevitable also that parameter estimates will have high standard errors and will be highly correlated. In fact, some model building studies seem to be exercises in inverting non-singular matrices!

(c) Given that model checking and criticism is seriously inadequate (see below), it follows that there is no mechanism by which such complex structures can be simplified when confronted with real world data, containing, as they often do, many sources of error.

It is perhaps salutory to remember that it is the hallmark of a good scientist that he is able to describe a wide range of phenomena and facts under the umbrella of simple models, containing few parameters. Thus, size and complexity of model structure is not a desirable objective – on the contrary, it is often indicative of mediocrity on the part of the model builder.

*Estimation.* All the information in the data about the parameters in a model, assuming that it is representationally adequate, is contained in the *likelihood function.* Therefore, understanding of the estimation situation resolves itself into a description of the likelihood function. It is possible to write down the exact likelihood function for the models described in the Appendices and to develop iterative estimation methods for arriving at the maximum likelihood estimates and their approximate covariance matrix. Therefore, there is no longer any need to 'force' models into a form whereby they can be treated by linear or multi-stage linear least squares. Such methods are unnecessary and inefficient.

*Checking.* Model checking, or criticism, is one of the most important aspects of model building in science. In fact, the distinction between science and non-science is determined by whether a proposition is *testable.* If it is not testable, then it may have more to do with theology than with science. Thus, model checking, that is looking for evidence of model inadequacy, (not model adequacy since no model can be 'adequate' in any absolute sense) forms a very important component of the methodology of science in general.

The main tool for checking econometric models is the Durbin–Watson test (Durbin & Watson, 1950, 1951; Durbin, 1970). Whereas this test has served a useful purpose in econometrics in the past, it is inadequate for transfer function-noise models since:

(a) it essentially looks at the first-lag autocorrelation $r_a(1)$ of the residuals – but model inadequacy may reside in the behaviour of the residual autocorrelations $r_a(k)$ for lags $k \geqslant 2$ and remain undetected by a Durbin–Watson test,

(b) more significantly, the absence of autocorrelation at any lag in the residuals is not in itself sufficient to conclude that the model is representationally adequate. As emphasized in previous sections, inadequacies in the transfer function (lag structure) can only be detected by cross correlating the residuals with each input series in turn. However, a highly autocorrelated input series can induce spurious cross correlation if correlated with the residual series, even if the latter is random. Hence, to enable the cross correlations to be interpreted unambiguously, it is necessary to prewhiten the inputs in turn before correlating with the residual series.

Since all models are 'wrong', small autocorrelations in the residuals and small cross correlations between the residuals and the prewhitened inputs, do not imply that the model is 'correct' in any sense. On the contrary, they mean that, given the finite length of series at the analyst's disposal, no serious inadequacies can be discovered. Given longer series, model inadequacies not apparent in the shorter series might then become more noticeable.

## 4.6. Forecasting

It is a matter for puzzlement to the writer that so many published forecasts do not:

(a) state clearly what *assumptions* are made in their generation,

(b) present, in addition to forecasts, limits which express the *uncertainty* in the forecasts,

(c) compare past forecasts with actual data when it comes to hand, that is, *monitor* the effectiveness of the forecasting system.

With respect to (a), if the user of the forecasts is not told what assumptions are being made concerning future values of the input variables, his understanding of the forecast is correspondingly diminished.

Concerning (b), no forecast is worth much without some measure of its uncertainty. In business forecasting, where the writer's experience mainly derives, it is the uncertainty in the forecast which is the major factor influencing a decision. Thus, in a situation where the *risk* associated with a decision is higher if for example the forecast is low rather than high, it is unlikely that the decision will be based on the so-called 'central' forecast*.

---

*In this connection, there is some confusion in the literature since some people have advocated that the estimation of the parameters in the model should take into account the fact that equal positive and negative forecast errors may have different financial (or other) consequences. However, this is a mistaken notion since the estimation situation is concerned with making probability statements about future forecast errors. Given the probability distribution of the forecast errors at different lead times, they can be combined with an appropriate *loss function*, if one can be formulated, to arrive at a decision rule — that is, the estimation and decision problem are logically distinct.

As far as (c) is concerned, forecasting should be seen as a *learning process*. Thus, forecast errors at different lead times should be systematically monitored so that past inadequacies can be uncovered and used as a basis for generating ideas as to how matters could be improved in the future.

*'Massaging' the residuals.* In econometric forecasting is it common practice to make assumptions about future values of the residuals. As discussed in Sections 2.3 and 3.3, if large residuals are caused by unusual events, such as strikes, holidays or other untypical events, then techniques such as intervention analysis can be used to take account of them. However, if the model building has been done efficiently, then the residuals should be consistent with the hypothesis that they are *random* with *mean zero* and a *constant standard deviation*. It is difficult to see how one can then specify the future values of a random series. If such a forecast of future residuals is attempted, it implies that they are not random — in which case the model was incorrect in the first place. If it is believed that certain variables will behave in the future in different ways from their behaviour in the past then such assumptions and judgements are more properly embodied in the behaviour of the explanatory or input variables. But to specify future values for the residuals seems to involve the use of statistical ideas not yet known to professional statisticians!

In contrast, the methods for forecasting considered in this publication (see Box and Jenkins, 1970, for forecasting univariate and transfer function models):

(a) involve the setting of future values of the random residuals to zero and the replacement of future values of measured variables by their forecasts,

(b) allow for the possibility of forecasts of the input variables to be made by a model of these input variables, or allow the user to specify external forecasts for these variables, or his own judgement,

(c) compute the standard deviations of the forecast errors at each future lead time,

(d) in the case of transfer function models, *combine* the errors due to the forecasting of the input variables with the errors in forecasting the noise to arrive at an overall measure of forecast accuracy.

# Appendices: Mathematical description of the five classes of model

The following sections contain a brief description of the five classes of model introduced in Part 2 and illustrated in Part 3. The all-important question of how to build these models is discussed only briefly here. Further details may be obtained from Box and Jenkins (1968, 1970) in the case of univariate and transfer function models. A brief description of model building for multivariate and intervention models is given in Appendices A.4, A.5 and A.6.

## A.1. Non-linear transformation of the data

Before analysing any statistical data, the first important decision that a statistician has to make is what *scale of measurement*, or transformation, should be used. Denoting the value of a time series at time $t$ by $z_t$, such a data transformation may be represented in general by $z_t^{(\lambda)}$ where $\lambda$ is a vector of parameters defining the transformation. The main objective of the transformation is to produce residuals in the fitted model that have a *constant variance\**. To first order of approximation the transformation has no other effect on the structure of the model. A particularly simple class of transformations which is frequently used is the class of power transformations defined by

$$z_t^{(\lambda)} = \begin{cases} z_t^{\lambda}, & \lambda \neq 0, \\ \ln z_t, & \lambda = 0. \end{cases}$$

However, other transformations could be considered.

*Range-mean plots.* The range-mean plot is a rough device for obtaining a preliminary estimate of the appropriate transformation to be applied to the data. It is calculated by first dividing the series into sub-sets (sub-sets of size say $4-12$

*Strictly speaking we require that the transformed residuals have a common probability distribution.

are useful for this purpose and ideally should be related to the size of the seasonal period) and calculating the *range* and *mean* of each sub-set. The plot of the range versus the mean of each sub-set is called the *range-mean plot*. The range of a sub-set is used in preference to the standard deviation as an estimate of local *variability* because of its simplicity; the mean is used as an estimate of the local *level* of the series.

If the range is independent of the mean, no transformation is needed ($\lambda = 1$) and the relationship between range and mean is a random scatter about a horizontal line as shown in Figure A.1.

A further useful transformation is the logarithmic transformation which is suggested if the range-mean plot displays random scatter about a straight line ($\lambda = 0$ in Figure A.1).

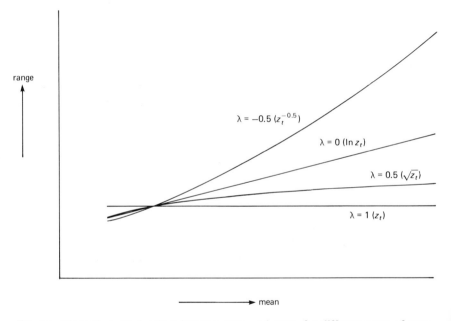

Fig A.1. Theoretical relationships between range and mean for different types of transformation (actual relationships based on data will display random scatter about these theoretical relationships).

A number of qualifications need to be made about the use of range-mean plots:

(1) it is a crude device and any real relationship could be swamped by random scatter,

(2) the objective is not to fix on precise values of $\lambda$, say $\lambda = 0.37$, but to distinguish between say $\lambda = 1, 0.5$ or $0$,

(3) some data sets are insensitive to the choice of $\lambda$, in which case the choice of transformation is not important. This situation can be recognised by the fact that the range-mean plots of the original and transformed data are very similar,

(4) some data sets may be moderately sensitive to transformation, in which case the range-mean plot should give some signal as to the choice of transformation,

(5) if it is felt that the data is very sensitive to transformation, the parameter $\lambda$ can be estimated along with other model parameters at the estimation stage of model building. A plot of the likelihood function of $\lambda$ will then indicate the sensitivity of the data to transformation. However, in this case also, unusual values of $\lambda$ should be avoided in order to make it easier to interpret the model and the forecasts.

## A.2. Univariate stochastic models

*Stationary models.* If the time series is stationary, that is, it is in statistical equilibrium about a constant mean $c$, it can be represented by a wide class of models, linear in the transformed variable, called autoregressive-moving average (ARMA) models, that is

$$(z_t^* - c) = \phi_1(z_{t-1}^* - c) - \ldots - \phi_p(z_{t-p}^* - c) + a_t - \theta_1 a_{t-1} - \ldots - \theta_q a_{t-q}$$

where $\quad z_t^* = z_t^{(\lambda)}$ . $\hspace{6cm}$ (A.1)

In words, the model represents the current value of the transformed series as a linear function of:

(a) past values of the transformed series $z_t^{(\lambda)}$,

(b) current and past values of the residuals $a_t$ (which may also be thought of as the one-step-ahead forecast errors of $z_t^{(\lambda)}$)

Alternatively, introducing the backward shift operator

$$Bz_t^* = z_{t-1}^*, \qquad B^j z_t^* = z_{t-j}^*,$$

$$Ba_t = a_{t-1}, \qquad B^j a_t = a_{t-j}$$

the ARMA model may be written in operator form as

$$z_t^{(\lambda)} - c = \frac{\theta(B)}{\phi(B)} = \frac{1 - \theta_1 B - \ldots - \theta_q B^q}{1 - \phi_1 B - \ldots - \phi_p B^p} a_t.$$ $\hspace{2cm}$ (A.2)

The parameters in (A.2) need to satisfy the following conditions:

(a) the roots (factors) of $\phi(B) = 0$ lie outside (inside) the unit circle for the autoregressive operator $\phi(B)$ to be *stationary* (series is in statistical equilibrium about a fixed mean),

(b) the roots (factors) of $\theta(B) = 0$ lie outside (inside) the unit circle for the moving average operator $\theta(B)$ to be *invertible* (weights applied to past history of series to generate forecasts die out).

The model (A.2) represents the transformed series $z_t^{(\lambda)}$ as the output from a *linear filter* whose input is a random series with zero mean and constant variance ('white noise') and whose filter transfer function is a ratio of two polynomials in the backward shift operator $B$. Writing the model in the form (A.2), and factorising the polynomials in $B$, greatly helps in understanding the mechanism generating the series. For example, complex factors correspond to some under- lying periodicity (with random changes in period, amplitude and phase), such as a business cycle.

To achieve *parsimony* in parameterisation, that is a representation which economises in the use of parameters, it is necessary in general to include both autoregressive and moving average terms in the model. In contrast, the use of an autoregressive model to represent a series which is described by a moving average model, or vice versa, will result in the prodigal use of parameters.

*Non-stationary models.* Whereas autoregressive models (Yule, 1927) and moving average models (Slutsky, 1927; Walker, 1931) have been known for some time, their use in time series modelling has been held up:

(a) because of the need to develop appropriate methods for identifying, fitting and checking these models,

(b) because inadequate methods existed for their use in describing *non- stationary* series, recourse usually being made to some arbitrary form of trend elimination before fitting an autoregressive or moving average model to the residuals after such a trend elimination procedure.

An important step forward in the description of non-stationary series is the recognition that a class of models, useful for representing a wide range of practical situations, is obtained by first differencing the transformed series $d$ times to induce stationarity, that is

$$w_t = \nabla^d z_t^{(\lambda)}. \tag{A.3a}$$

The stationary series $w_t$ can then be represented by an ARMA model

$$w_t - c = \frac{\theta(B)}{\phi(B)} a_t = \frac{1 - \theta_1 B - \ldots - \theta_q B^q}{1 - \phi_1 B - \ldots - \phi_p B^p} a_t. \tag{A.3b}$$

The model defined by (A.3a) and (A.3b) is called an Autoregressive Integrated Moving Average model or ARIMA $(p, d, q)$ model (Box and Jenkins, 1962, 1967). Yaglom (1955) has independently described models involving differencing as *accumulated processes*. Such models are capable of describing a wide class of *stochastic trends*, whose coefficients *adapt* as each observation comes to hand. Thus, models involving single differencing $\nabla$ can be used to describe series whose *level* is continuously updated by random shocks; models involving double differencing $\nabla^2$ can describe series whose *level* and *slope* are continuously updated by random shocks, and so on. Usually, single differencing is adequate to describe most non-stationary series but occasionally double differencing may be necessary.

*Seasonal models.* To describe series containing seasonal patterns with period $s$, and which may also be evolving in a non-stationary manner, a new class of models (Box, Jenkins and Bacon, 1967) has been developed. Thus, the seasonal $(p, d, q) \times (P, D, Q)_s$ model is defined by

$$w_t = \nabla^d \nabla_s^D z_t^{(\lambda)},$$

$$w_t - c = \frac{\theta(B)\theta(B^s)}{\phi(B)\Phi(B^s)} a_t \qquad (A.4)$$

where $\phi(B)$, $\theta(B)$ are non-seasonal autoregressive and moving average operators, as defined in (A.2),

$$\nabla_s z_t^{(\lambda)} = z_t^{(\lambda)} - z_{t-s}^{(\lambda)}$$

is the seasonal differencing operator, and

$$\Phi(B^s) = 1 - \Phi_1 B^s - \Phi_2 B^{2s} - \cdots - \Phi_P^{Ps},$$

$$\Theta(B^s) = 1 - \Theta_1 B^s - \Theta_2 B^{2s} - \cdots - \Theta_Q B^{Qs}$$

are seasonal autoregressive and moving average operators. The seasonal model (A.4) is capable of representing a wide class of stochastic trends and stochastic seasonal patterns, such as occur in practice, under the umbrella of one *single model*.

In addition, the constant $c$, which measures the mean of the appropriately transformed and differenced series $w_t$, can be used to describe a wide class of deterministic functions of time, should prior knowledge, or the model building process, suggest that they be included.

If necessary, the model (A.4), which is *multiplicative* with respect to its non-seasonal and seasonal components, may be replaced by a *non-multiplicative* model if there are indications that this elaboration is necessary at the identification stage of model building (see Box and Jenkins, 1970). Furthermore, in some problems it may be necessary to include several seasonal periods. For example, energy data may display a cycle over a day, a further cycle over a week and yet a further cycle over a year. Such multiple seasonality can be described by elaborating (A.4) so as to include further stages of seasonal differencing and further seasonal autoregressive and moving average operators.

Figure A.2 shows the filter representation of the seasonal model (A.4) and Figure A.3 a flow diagram for building univariate models. For further details of univariate stochastic model building, see Box and Jenkins (1970).

## A.3. Transfer function models

For illustration, suppose that there is one output variable $Y_t$ which is to be forecast and one input variable which is to be related to the variable to be forecast. Then, as indicated in Figure A.4, $Y_t$ may be split into two components:

$$Y_t = U_t + N_t \tag{A.5}$$

where

$U_t$ contains that part of $Y_t$ which can be explained exactly in terms of $X_t$,

$N_t$ is an error or *noise* term which can not be explained in terms of $X_t$ – it represents all the 'missing' $X$-variables.

We consider first the relationship between $U_t$ and the input $X_t$. A general way of representing a linear dynamic relationship of this kind is

$$U_t - \delta_1 U_{t-1} - \cdots - \delta_r U_{t-r} = \omega_0 X_{t-b} - \omega_1 X_{t-b-1} - \cdots - \omega_s X_{t-b-s}$$

that is

$$U_t = \frac{\omega_0 - \omega_1 B - \cdots - \omega_s B^s}{1 - \delta_1 B - \cdots - \delta_r B^r} X_{t-b} = \frac{\omega(B)}{\delta(B)} X_{t-b} = v(B) X_t$$

where

$$v(B) = \frac{\omega(B)}{\delta(B)} B^b$$

The *transfer function* $v(B)$ contains
   (i) a 'moving average' operator $\omega(B)$,
   (ii) an 'autoregressive' operator $\delta(B)$,
   (iii) a *pure delay* parameter $b$, which represents the number of complete time intervals before a change in $X_t$ *begins* to have an effect on $Y_t$.

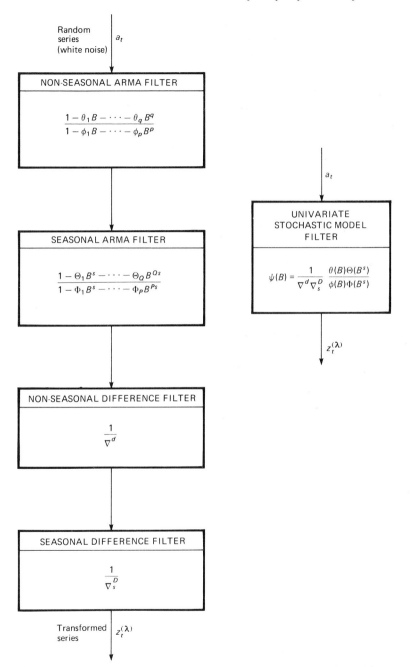

Fig A.2. Filter representation of multiplicative seasonal univariate stochastic model.

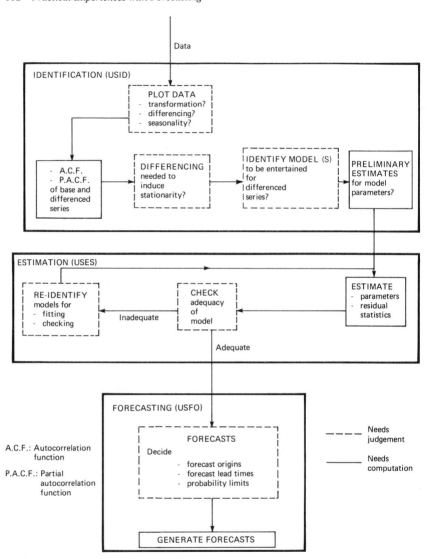

Fig A.3. Flow diagram for univariate stochastic model building and forecasting, based on three computer programs: USID (Univariate Stochastic Identification Program), USES (Univariate Stochastic Estimation Program), USFO (Univariate Stochastic Forecasting Program).

In general, *non-statistical considerations* may dictate that we relate a differenced output $Y_t$ to a possibly differently differenced input $X_t$. For example, we might want to relate $Y_t$ to the rate of change of $X_t$, that is $\nabla X_t$. If, in addition, we allow for the need to transform the variables, (A.5) may be written more generally as

$$\nabla^d Y_t^{(\lambda_Y)} = U_t + N_t$$

$$= \frac{\omega(B)}{\delta(B)} \nabla^{d_1} X_{t-b}^{(\lambda_X)} + N_t. \tag{A.6}$$

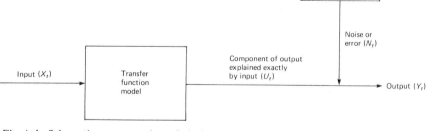

Fig A.4. Schematic representation of single output, single input transfer function—noise model.

In general, the noise will be non-stationary and hence in many practical situations could be represented by an ARIMA $(p, d, q)$ model of the form (A.3), that is

$$\nabla^{d_N} N_t = c + \frac{\theta(B)}{\phi(B)} a_t. \tag{A.7}$$

On eliminating $N_t$ between (A.6) and (A.7), we obtain a *transfer function-noise model*

$$y_t = c + \frac{\omega(B)}{\delta(B)} x_{t-b} + \frac{\theta(B)}{\phi(B)} a_t \tag{A.8}$$

where

$$y_t = \nabla^{dY} Y_t^{(\lambda Y)}, \qquad dY = d + dN,$$

$$x_t = \nabla^{dX} X_t^{(\lambda X)}, \qquad dX = d_1 + dN.$$

Proceeding as in ordinary regression analysis, the estimation of the constant $c$ can be made approximately orthogonal to the other model parameters if the $x$-series is mean corrected, that is

$$y_t = c + \frac{\omega(B)}{\delta(B)} (x_{t-b} - \bar{x}) + \frac{\theta(B)}{\phi(B)} a_t. \qquad (A.9)$$

*Multiple input models.* If several input variables $X_{1t}, X_{2t}, \ldots, X_{lt}$ are to be related to the output $Y_t$, then (A.9) may be generalised to

$$y_t = c + \sum_{j=1}^{l} \frac{\omega_j(B)}{\delta_j(B)} (x_{j,t-b_j} - \bar{x}_j) + \frac{\theta(B)}{\phi(B)} a_t \qquad (A.10)$$

each $X$-variable having a transfer function with its own moving average operator $\omega_j(B)$, autoregressive operator $\delta_j(B)$ and pure delay $b_j$.

*Seasonal models.* Finally, if $Y_t$ and the $X_{it}$ are seasonal series with seasonal period $s$, we obtain a seasonal transfer function model

$$\nabla^d Y_t^{(\lambda Y)} = \sum_{j=1}^{l} \frac{\omega_j(B)}{\delta_j(B)} \nabla^{d_j} X_{jt}^{(\lambda X_{j,t})} + N_t$$

where

$$\nabla^{dN} \nabla_s^{DN} N_t = \frac{\theta(B)\Theta(B^S)}{\phi(B)\Phi(B^S)} a_t. \qquad (A.11)$$

The model (A.11) can also be written in the form (A.10) with suitable definition of $y_t, x_t$ and the inclusion of seasonal operators in the noise.

Figure A.5 shows a filter representation of the seasonal multiple input transfer function model (A.11) and Figure A.6 a flow diagram for building transfer function models. For further details of transfer function model building, see Box and Jenkins (1970).

## A.4. Intervention models

During the course of building the four main types of model described in these Appendices, it may be necessary to introduce further modifications to the model

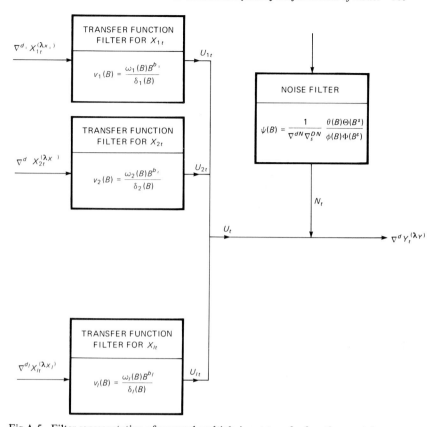

Fig A.5. Filter representation of seasonal multiple input transfer function model.

to deal with abnormal events or other forms of effects which are not easy to quantify. The following *dummy variables* are useful for representing such behaviour:

(i) *pulse* variables, which take on the value '1' when an anomalous event (such as a holiday or a strike) occurs and are '0' everywhere else,

(ii) *step* variables, which take on the value '0' *before* a change (such as a policy change, or a new law, or a change in definition in an economic variable) and the value '1' *after* such a change.

To investigate the effect of such an intervention variable $\xi_t$ on the variable being modelled, we may postulate a lag structure

$$Y_t^{(\lambda)} = \frac{\omega(B)}{\delta(B)} \xi_{t-b} \tag{A.12}$$

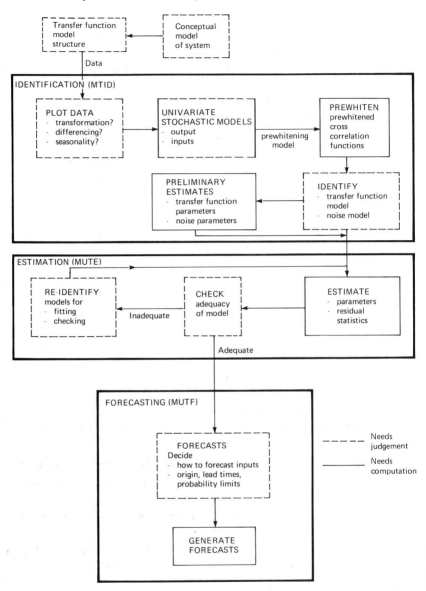

**Fig A.6.** Flow diagram for transfer function model building and forecasting, based on three computer programs: MTID (Multiple Input Transfer Function Identification), MUTE (Multiple Input Transfer Function Estimation), MUTF (Multiple Input Transfer Function Forecasting).

whose parameters can be estimated as in a transfer function model.

It is not possible to use prewhitening to identify the structure of an intervention model (A.12) as in the case of transfer function models. Instead the following guidelines may be used in complement with each other to identify intervention models:

(1) As a result of a known external event, inspection of the data itself may suggest ways in which that event has changed the course of the series. For example, inspection of many consumer price indices will indicate that their rate of change has increased as a result of the dramatic oil price increase in the last quarter of 1973. This effect can be modelled by introducing an intervention term into an existing model as follows:

$$\nabla Y_t^{(\lambda)} = \omega_0 \xi_t \tag{A.13}$$

where $\xi_t$ is a step function jumping from '0' to '1' at the point of the so-called 'oil crisis'.

(2) Supplementary evidence may also be obtained by examining the residuals from the model fitted before an intervention variable is introduced. For example, a large negative residual followed by a large positive residual in a univariate model may be due to a loss of sales during the period of a 'strike' and a catching up in deliveries in the period following the strike. Such an effect may be described by the model:

$$Y_t^{(\lambda)} = (\omega_0 - \omega_1 B)\xi_t \tag{A.14}$$

where $\xi_t$ is a pulse of unit height at the point where the strike occurred.

(3) Whereas (1) and (2) are useful in providing visual clues that an abnormal change has taken place in a series, a better way to postulate an intervention model is to discuss the *mechanisms* that might be causing the change with those who have some understanding of the situation being considered. If the postulated model is too elaborate, those parameters which are small compared with their standard errors in the fitted model can be omitted and the simpler model fitted. Alternatively, if it is suspected that the model is inadequate, further terms can be added. Figure A.7 shows further examples of the effects on the $Y_t$ variables in (A.12) which can be modelled by simple transfer function models when the intervention variable $\xi_t$ is a step or pulse.

*Introducing the noise into an intervention model.* To complete the specification of an intervention model, it is necessary to assume a structure for the behaviour of the series that would have occurred if no abnormal event had taken place.

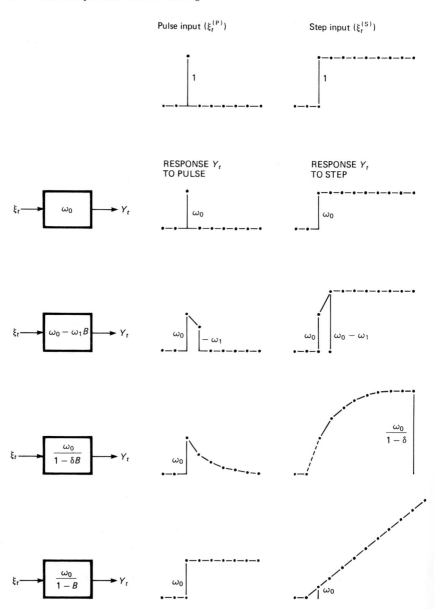

Fig A.7. Examples of dynamic effects which can be simulated in intervention analysis using a 'pulse' input and step input.

To illustrate the approach, suppose that a univariate model:

$$\nabla\nabla_{12}Y_t^{(\lambda)} = (1 - \theta B)(1 - \Theta B^{12})a_t \tag{A.15}$$

had been fitted to a series, preferably to data not including the period when the abnormal event occurred. Then, if the intervention mechanism was (A.14), we could postulate a model

$$Y_t^{(\lambda)} = (\omega_0 - \omega_1 B)\xi_t + N_t \tag{A.16}$$

where $N_t$ is a noise term describing the behaviour of the series in the absence of the abnormal event. If $\omega_0$ and $\omega_1$ were both zero in (A.16) then $Y_t^{(\lambda)} = N_t$. Hence, we can use the univariate model (A.15) for $Y_t^{(\lambda)}$ as a first guess of the structure of $N_t$, that is

$$\nabla\nabla_{12}N_t = (1 - \theta B)(1 - \Theta B^{12})a_t. \tag{A.17}$$

Combining (A.17) with (A.16), we obtain the overall intervention model

$$\nabla\nabla_{12}Y_t^{(\lambda)} = (\omega_0 - \omega_1 B)\nabla\nabla_{12}\xi_t + (1 - \theta B)(1 - \Theta B^{12})a_t.$$

In contrast, the intervention model corresponding to the mechanism (A.13) could be formulated as

$$\nabla Y_t^{(\lambda)} = \omega_0\xi_t + N_t'. \tag{A.18}$$

Again, setting $\omega_0 = 0$, the initial structure for $N_t'$ could be set equal to the structure of $\nabla Y_t^{(\lambda)}$. Using (A.15), this is

$$\nabla_{12}N_t' = (1 - \theta B)(1 - \Theta B^{12})a_t. \tag{A.19}$$

Combining (A.18) with (A.19), we obtain the overall intervention model

$$\nabla\nabla_{12}Y_t^{(\lambda)} = \omega_0\nabla_{12}\xi_t + (1 - \theta B)(1 - \Theta B^{12})a_t.$$

Further examples of identifying intervention models are given in Section 3.3.

In general, several terms of the form (A.12) may need to be introduced into one of the models described in these Appendices. For example, a pulse may be needed at several points to allow for the effect of different holidays on energy consumption.

## A.5. Multivariate stochastic models

Pioneering work in the area of multivariate stochastic models was carried out by Bartlett (1950, 1953) and Quenouille (1957). Quenouille's approach was to generalise the univariate autoregressive-moving average models of Appendix A.2 to

$$\phi_0 z_t = \phi_1 z_{t-1} + \cdots + \phi_p z_{t-p} + \theta_0 a_t - \theta_1 a_{t-1} - \cdots - \theta_q a_{t-q} \qquad (A.20)$$

where $z_t$ is a column vector whose transpose $z_t' = (z_{1t}, z_{2t}, \ldots, z_{mt})$ is a row vector of $m$ time series, the $\phi_i$ and $\theta_j$ are $m \times m$ autoregressive and moving average matrices respectively and the elements $a_{it}$ of the vector $a_t$ are mutually uncorrelated at all times. Whereas, the Quenouille model (A.20) provides a useful starting point, it suffers from two practical disadvantages:

(i) The formulation in (A.20) constrains the univariate models for the individual time series $z_{it}$ to have autoregressive operators which

(a) have the same order,

(b) have the same parameter values.

This constraint is highly undesirable and can be removed by writing the model in the form (Alavi, 1973)

$$\begin{bmatrix} \phi_{11}(B) & \phi_{12}(B) \cdots \phi_{1m}(B) \\ \phi_{21}(B) & \phi_{22}(B) \cdots \phi_{2m}(B) \\ \cdot & \cdot \quad \cdots \quad \cdot \\ \cdot & \cdot \quad \cdots \quad \cdot \\ \cdot & \cdot \quad \cdots \quad \cdot \\ \phi_{m1}(B) & \phi_{m2}(B) \quad \phi_{mm}(B) \end{bmatrix} \begin{bmatrix} z_{1t} - c_1 \\ z_{2t} - c_2 \\ \cdot \\ \cdot \\ \cdot \\ z_{mt} - c_m \end{bmatrix} = \begin{bmatrix} \theta_{11}(B) \, \theta_{12}(B) \cdots \theta_{1m}(B) \\ \theta_{21}(B) \, \theta_{22}(B) \cdots \theta_{2m}(B) \\ \cdot \quad \cdot \quad \cdots \quad \cdot \\ \cdot \quad \cdot \quad \cdots \quad \cdot \\ \cdot \quad \cdot \quad \cdots \quad \cdot \\ \theta_{m1}(B) \, \theta_{m2}(B) \ldots \theta_{mm}(B) \end{bmatrix} \begin{bmatrix} a_{1t} \\ a_{2t} \\ \cdot \\ \cdot \\ \cdot \\ a_{mt} \end{bmatrix}$$

or
$$\phi(B)(z_t - c) = \theta(B) a_t \qquad (A.21)$$

where the autoregressive operator $\phi_{ij}(B)$ is a polynomial of degree $p_{ij}$ in the backward shift operator $B$ and the moving average operator $\theta_{ij}(B)$ is a polynomial of degree $q_{ij}$ in $B$. As in previous models, the time series $z_{it}$ in the vector $z_t$ in (A.21) may need to be transformed to $z_{it}^{(\lambda_i)}$ before analysis.

In (A.21) the polynomials in the diagonal positions start with unity while the polynomials in the off-diagonal positions start with a power of $B$. With this formulation, the $a_{it}$ are the one-step-ahead forecast errors which then must be allowed to have a covariance matrix at simultaneous times

$$\Sigma = \begin{bmatrix} \sigma_1^2 & \sigma_{12} \cdots \sigma_{1m} \\ \sigma_{21} & \sigma_2^2 \cdots \sigma_{2m} \\ \sigma_{m1} & \sigma_{m2} \ldots \sigma_m^2 \end{bmatrix} \qquad (A.22)$$

with $\sigma_{ij} = \sigma_{ji}$, but are otherwise mutually uncorrelated at non-simultaneous times.

The model (A.21) will be referred to as a multivariate autoregressive-moving average model or ARMA $(P, Q)$ model. During the model building process the degrees of the operators $\phi_{ij}(B)$ and $\theta_{ij}(B)$ can be adjusted so that the univariate models for the individual time series accurately describe the behaviour of each series and are not automatically constrained as in the model (A.20).

(ii) A further disadvantage of the model (A.20) is that it assumes stationarity, that is the $m$ time series are in statistical equilibrium about fixed means. To describe series which have stochastic trends, the model (A.21) may be generalised to

$$\phi(B)(w_t - c) = \theta(B) a_t$$

where (A.23)

$$w_t' = (\nabla^{d_1} z_{1t}^{(\lambda_1)}, \ldots, \nabla^{d_m} z_{mt}^{(\lambda_m)})$$

with $\phi(B)$ and $\theta(B)$ as defined in (A.21) and $c$ a vector of constants. Such a model will be referred to as a *multivariate* ARIMA $(P, d, Q)$ model, where the matrices $P = (p_{ij})$, $Q = (q_{ij})$ determine the degrees of the polynomials in the autoregressive and moving average matrices and the row vector $d' = (d_1, d_2, \ldots, d_m)$ has elements corresponding to the degrees of differencing required to induce stationarity in each of the individual time series.

*Seasonal multivariate stochastic models.* As for univariate and transfer function models it may be necessary to difference a series both seasonally as well as non-seasonally to induce stationarity. Thus the elements $w_{it}$ of the vector $w_t$ in (A.23) will need to be defined as

$$w_{it} = \nabla^{d_i} \nabla_s^{D_i} z_{it}^{(\lambda_i)}.$$ (A.24)

One possible way to introduce seasonality into the main part of the multivariate stochastic model (A.23) is to write the autoregressive and moving average matrices as products of non-seasonal and seasonal matrices, by analogy with the univariate case (A.4). However, certain theoretical difficulties have been experienced with this formulation. The way in which this problem has been resolved in practice is to allow the autoregressive and moving average operators in the matrices in (A.23) to be non-multiplicative. Thus, the computer programs necessary for building multivariate stochastic models have been written to allow an autoregressive operator $\phi_{ij}(B)$ in (A.21) to be written, for example, as

$$\phi_{ij}(B) = 1 - \phi_{ij,1} B - \phi_{ij,12} B^{12} - \phi_{ij,13} B^{13}$$

if there is seasonality of 12 present. By allowing parameters to be inserted at any particular lag in the operator, greater flexibility can be obtained. Figure A.8 shows a filter representation of a multivariate stochastic model.

*Stationarity and invertibility conditions.* As for univariate stochastic models (See Section A.2), the parameters in the multivariate stochastic model (A.23) need to satisfy certain conditions. For the multivariate case, these conditions are as follows:

(i) With the differencing (A.24) applied to induce stationarity, the parameters in the autoregressive matrix $\phi(B)$ in (A.23) must satisfy the condition that the *factors* of the determinantal equation

$$|\phi(B)| = 0 \qquad\qquad (A.25)$$

lie inside the unit circle, or the *roots* of (A.25) lie outside the unit circle. The *stationarity condition* (A.25) ensures that the statistical properties of the differenced series are time invariant, that is in some form of statistical equilibrium.

(ii) The parameters in the moving average matrix $\theta(B)$ in (A.23) must satisfy the condition that the factors of

$$|\theta(B)| = 0 \qquad\qquad (A.26)$$

lie inside the unit circle, or the roots of (A.26) lie outside the unit circle. The *invertibility condition* (A.26) ensures that if the model (A.23) is used to generate simultaneous forecasts of the transformed series $z_{it}^{(\lambda)}$, the weights applied to previous observations will die out as we stretch further into the past — as should happen for any sensible forecast.

*Uncorrelated residual form of model.* The model (A.23) is capable of being written in several alternative forms. For example, instead of allowing the residuals $a_{it}$ to be cross correlated at simultaneous times, with covariance matrix $\Sigma$ as given by (A.22), it is possible to transform the model so that the transformed residuals $a_{it}^*$ are mutually uncorrelated at *all* times. Thus, if $\Lambda$ is the diagonal matrix of latent roots of $\Sigma$, and $U$ the matrix whose columns are the right hand latent vectors of $\Sigma$, the transformation

$$a_t^* = U a_t$$

will convert the correlated vector $a_t$ into the uncorrelated vector $a_t^*$. Applying the inverse transformation $a_t = U' a_t^*$ to (A.23), we obtain

$$\phi(B)(w_t - c) = \theta^*(B) a_t^* \qquad\qquad (A.27)$$

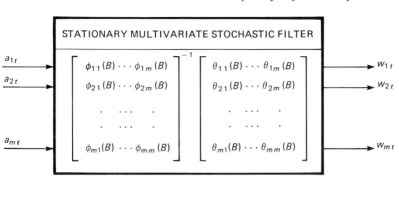

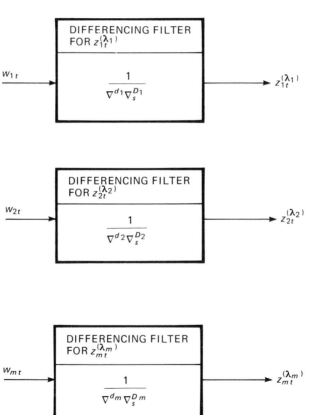

Fig A.8. *Filter representation of seasonal multivariate stochastic model.*

where $\boldsymbol{\theta}*(B) = \boldsymbol{\theta}(B)U'$. Whereas the polynomials $\theta_{ij}(B)$ making up the elements of $\boldsymbol{\theta}(B)$ start with a '1' on the diagonals and a term in $B$ on the off-diagonals, the polynomials $\theta_{ij}^*(B)$ in $\boldsymbol{\theta}*(B)$ can begin with a term in $B^0 = 1$ at any point in the matrix.

*Coupled transfer function form of model.* Yet another alternative form is obtained when (A.27) is written as

$$a_t^* = \frac{[\text{adj. } \boldsymbol{\theta}*(B)]\boldsymbol{\phi}(B)(w_t - c)}{|\boldsymbol{\theta}*(B)|}$$

$$= \boldsymbol{\phi}*(B)(w_t - c) \tag{A.28}$$

where

$$\boldsymbol{\phi}*(B) = \frac{[\text{adj. } \boldsymbol{\theta}*(B)]\boldsymbol{\phi}(B)}{|\boldsymbol{\theta}*(B)|}$$

and $[\text{adj. } \boldsymbol{\theta}*(B)]$ denotes the adjoint matrix of the matrix $\boldsymbol{\theta}*(B)$.
The $i$th equation in (A.28) may be written as

$$(w_{it} - c_i) = -\frac{\phi_{i1}^*(B)}{\phi_{ii}^*(B)}(w_{1t} - c_1) - \cdots - \frac{\phi_{im}^*(B)}{\phi_{ii}^*(B)}(w_{mt} - c_m) + a_{it}^*.$$

In this form, the model is represented as a set of coupled transfer functions with $w_{1t}, w_{2t}, \ldots, w_{mt}$ in turn as outputs. Writing the model in this form can sometimes help to obtain a better understanding of the situation. For example, when $m = 2$

$$(w_{1t} - c_1) = -\frac{\phi_{12}^*(B)}{\phi_{11}^*(B)}(w_{2t} - c_2) + \frac{1}{\phi_{11}^*(B)}a_{1t}^*,$$

$$(w_{2t} - c_2) = -\frac{\phi_{21}^*(B)}{\phi_{22}^*(B)}(w_{1t} - c_1) + \frac{1}{\phi_{22}^*(B)}a_{2t}^*$$

and the model is represented as a pair of coupled transfer functions – a 'forward' transfer function relating $w_{1t}$ to $w_{2t}$ and a 'backward' transfer function relating $w_{2t}$ to $w_{1t}$. This form of the multivariate stochastic model is related to one used by Granger and Newbold (1976, 1977).

*Uncoupled form of model.* As a further step in obtaining a better understanding of the model, it is sometimes useful to express it in terms of *canonical variables*. The canonical variables consist of linear combinations of the original variables possessing simpler autocorrelation functions than the original variables. The method of canonical transformation given here is a generalisation of a method given by Quenouille (1957). To perform this canonical analysis we write the model (A.23) in the form

$$w_t = \phi_1 w_{t-1} + \cdots + \phi_p w_{t-p} + u_t \tag{A.29}$$

where $u_t = \theta(B)a_t$ and for convenience it is assumed that $c \equiv 0$. (A.29) may now be written in *state-vector* form as

$$
\begin{bmatrix} w_t \\ w_{t-1} \\ . \\ . \\ . \\ w_{t-p+1} \end{bmatrix}
=
\begin{bmatrix} \phi_1 & \phi_2 & \cdots & \phi_{p-1} & \phi_p \\ I & 0 & \cdots & 0 & 0 \\ . & . & & . & \\ . & . & & . & \\ . & . & & . & \\ 0 & 0 & \cdots & I & 0 \end{bmatrix}
\begin{bmatrix} w_{t-1} \\ w_{t-2} \\ . \\ . \\ . \\ w_{t-p} \end{bmatrix}
+
\begin{bmatrix} U_t \\ 0 \\ . \\ . \\ . \\ 0 \end{bmatrix}
$$

or

$$w_t^* = \phi^* w_{t-1} + u_t^* \tag{A.30}$$

If $\Lambda$ is the diagonal matrix of latent roots of $\phi^*$ and $B$ is the matrix whose columns are the right hand latent vectors of $\phi^*$, the form (A.30) of the model may be transformed to

$$y_t = \Lambda y_{t-1} + v_t \tag{A.31}$$

where

$$y_t = B^{-1} w_t^*, \qquad v_t = B^{-1} u_t^*,$$

For example, suppose that the uncoupled form of the model is the first-order autoregressive model

$$w_t = \phi w_{t-1} + a_t$$

where

$$\phi = -\frac{1}{12}\begin{bmatrix} 5 & -1 \\ 2 & 2 \end{bmatrix}.$$

Then

$$\Lambda = -\frac{1}{12}\begin{bmatrix} 4 & 0 \\ 0 & 3 \end{bmatrix},$$

$$B = \begin{bmatrix} 1 & 1 \\ 1 & 2 \end{bmatrix}, \qquad B^{-1} = \begin{bmatrix} 2 & -1 \\ -1 & 1 \end{bmatrix}$$

Hence, the canonical variables are

$$y_{1t} = 2w_{1t} - w_{2t},$$
$$y_{2t} = -w_{1t} + w_{2t}$$

which have the following uncoupled representations:

$$y_{1t} = -\frac{4}{12} y_{1,t-1} + 2a_{1t} - a_{2t},$$

$$y_{2t} = -\frac{3}{12} y_{2,t-1} - a_{1t} + a_{2t}.$$

An interesting form of canonical analysis, which is different from the above, has recently been given by Box and Tiao (1977).

*Aligned models.* It sometimes happens that external shocks which affect one time series may affect another time series after a delay. As a result, the cross correlation function between the two time series may be centred at a lag other than zero. If the model (A.23) is fitted to series of this kind, it may contain more parameters than are really necessary. To obtain a more parsimonious representation, a device, useful in spectral analysis (See Jenkins and Watts, 1968, pp. 399, 400), called *alignment* may be used. In practice, this means that initial guesses of the alignment parameters can be obtained by shifting the time series forwards or backwards relative to each other until the cross correlation functions are approximately centred at zero. If necessary, the alignment parameters can be estimated more precisely during the estimation stage of the model building process.

*Model building.* Figure A.9 shows a flow diagram for building multivariate stochastic models. As for previous models, the model building is carried out in three stages: identification, estimation and checking. As in Figure A.6, it is useful to build a conceptual model of the system under study before embarking upon the time series modelling. An example of such a conceptual model is given in Figure 4. The first step in the identification stage is to identify, fit and check univariate stochastic models for each series separately.

Suppose that these univariate models are represented by

$$w_{it} = \psi_i(B)\alpha_{it}$$

or in matrix form

$$w_t = \psi(B)\alpha_t \tag{A.32}$$

where the matrix $\psi(B)$ is diagonal with elements $\psi_i(B)$. The next step is to calculate the cross correlation function $r_{ij}(k)$ between each pair of residual series $\alpha_{it}$ and $\alpha_{jt}$. These correlations will be called the prewhitened cross correlation functions (c.c.f.'s). As in the univariate case, we may also calculate a set of partial cross correlations $s_{ij}(k)$ between each pair of residual series. The patterns in the prewhitened correlations $r_{ij}(k)$ and $s_{ij}(k)$ may then be used to identify:

(i) the degrees of alignment needed to centre the c.c.f.'s about zero,

(ii) a model

$$\alpha_t = \psi_1(B)a_t \tag{A.33}$$

for the aligned residuals,

(iii) an overall model

$$w_t = \psi(B)\psi_1(B)a_t \tag{A.34}$$

for the appropriately transformed, differenced and aligned series $w_t$.

At the estimation stage, the parameters in the identified model (A.34) are estimated by fully efficient maximum likelihood methods, together with their standard errors, and their correlation matrix. Also estimated is the covariance matrix $\Sigma$ whose elements are the covariances between the residuals $a_{it}$ at simultaneous times. (Wilson, 1973; Box, Hillner and Tiao, 1976).

At the checking stage the residuals $a_{it}$ are plotted as time series, together with 'control limits' $\pm 2\sigma_i$. Action can then be taken to investigate the causes of unusually large residuals and to establish whether they are caused by *known* abnormal events which can be modelled by intervention variables. In addition, the auto- and cross correlations of the residuals need to be examined to see whether they reveal model inadequacy. Large values compared with their standard errors in the correlation function $r_{ij}(k)$ will usually indicate model inadequacy in the $(j,i)$ positions in the autoregressive or moving average matrices. It should be remembered, however, that cross correlations $r_{ij}(k)$ may be present at lag $k = 0$ even if the model is adequate since these correlations are an integral part of the model. This is so because $\hat{\sigma}_i\hat{\sigma}_j r_{ij}(0)$ is an estimate of the elements $\sigma_{ij}$ in the covariance matrix $\Sigma$ given by (A.22). If there is any evidence of model inadequacy in the residual auto- and cross correlation functions, then a model can be identified for the residuals, combined with the original model, as described above, and then the overall model fitted and subsequently checked.

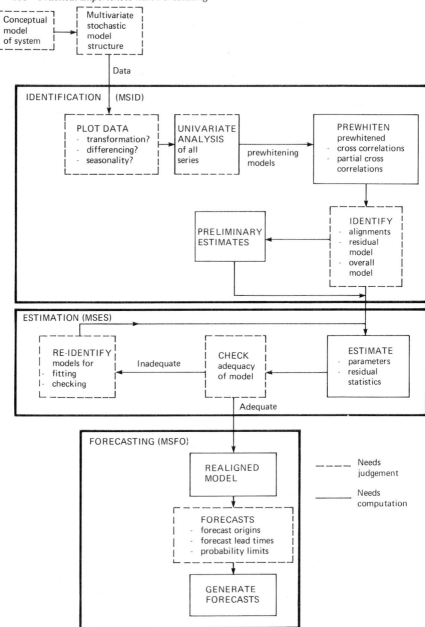

Fig A.9. Flow diagram for multivariate stochastic model building based on three computer programs: MSID (Multivariate Stochastic Identification), MSES (Multivariate Stochastic Estimation), MSFO (Multivariate Stochastic Forecasting).

At the forecasting stage, the model may have to be re-aligned (shifted back into real time) if alignment was needed in the first place. Then, on specification of the origin of the forecast, its lead time and the probability limits required, the forecasts can be generated, together with the covariance matrix of the forecast errors at each lead time.

An application of building multivariate stochastic models is given in Section 3.4 and also in Jenkins (1974).

*A.6. Multivariate transfer function models*

In this case we consider the relationship between $l$ input variables

$$X_{1t}, X_{2t}, \ldots, X_{lt}$$

and $m$ output variables

$$Y_{1t}, Y_{2t}, \ldots, Y_{mt}.$$

The transfer function for a single output may be written, as in Section A.3, as

$$\nabla^{dY_i} Y_{it}^{(\lambda Y_i)} = \sum_{j=1}^{l} \frac{\omega_j(B)}{\delta_j(B)} B^{b_{ij}} \nabla^{dX_j} X_{jt}^{(\lambda X_j)} + N_{it} \tag{A.35}$$

The single output models may then be coupled together by assuming that the noise series $N_{it}$ follow a multivariate stochastic model (A.23) with seasonal differencing as defined in (A.24). Figure A.10 shows the filter representation of the model.

Substituting for the multivariate noise model, and correcting for the means of the $X$-series, the model may be written in the more convenient form

$$y_{it} = c_i + \sum_{j=1}^{l} \frac{\omega_{ij}(B)}{\delta_{ij}(B)} B^{b_{ij}} (x_{ij,t} - \bar{x}_{ij}) + n_{it}. \tag{A.36}$$

where

$$x_{ij,t} = \nabla^{dX_{ij}} \nabla_s^{DX_{ij}} X_{jt}^{(\lambda X_j)}$$

and $\bar{x}_{ij}$ is the mean of the $x_{ij,t}$ series. The degrees of differencing $dX_{ij}$ and $DX_{ij}$ are determined by the degrees of differencing to be associated with the variable $X_{jt}$ in the model and the degrees of differencing associated with the noise $N_{it}$, as explained in relation to (A.8).

The equations (A.36) for $i = 1, 2, \ldots, m$ can also be assembled in matrix form as

$$y_t = c + v(B) \otimes \nabla (X_t - \bar{X}) + n_t \tag{A.37}$$

where $\otimes$ denotes the Kronecker (or direct) product of two matrices, the *transfer function matrix* $v(B)$ is given by

$$v(B) = \begin{bmatrix} \dfrac{\omega_{11}(B)}{\delta_{11}(B)} B^{b_{11}} & \dfrac{\omega_{12}(B)}{\delta_{12}(B)} B^{b_{12}} & \cdots & \dfrac{\omega_{1l}(B)}{\delta_{1l}(B)} B^{b_{1l}} \\ \cdot & \cdot & \cdots & \\ \dfrac{\omega_{m1}(B)}{\delta_{m1}(B)} B^{b_{m1}} & \dfrac{\omega_{m2}(B)}{\delta_{m2}(B)} B^{b_{m2}} & \cdots & \dfrac{\omega_{ml}(B)}{\delta_{ml}(B)} B^{b_{ml}} \end{bmatrix}$$

$y_t$ is a vector whose elements are the degrees of differencing to be applied to the $Y_{it}$ series by combining the differencing in (A.35) with the differencing applied to the noise $N_{it}$, the matrix $\nabla$ has elements $\nabla^{d X_{ij}} \nabla_s^{D X_{ij}}$ and $X_t$ is the vector whose elements are $X_{it}^{(\lambda X_i)}$.

Finally, the stationary noise vector $n_t$ can be represented by the multivariate stochastic model (A.21)

$$\phi(B)n_t = \theta(B)a_t$$

On substitution in (A.37), we obtain

$$y_t = c + v(B) \otimes \nabla(X_t - \bar{X}) + \phi^{-1}(B)\theta(B)a_t. \tag{A.38}$$

The model (A.38) provides a very flexible means of relating non-stationary, seasonal series by means of a transfer function matrix, which enables the lag structures to be coupled, and autoregressive and moving average matrices, which enable the noise structure to be coupled.

*Model building.* Figure A.11 is a flow diagram for building multivariate transfer function models, based on three stages: identification, estimation and checking. As emphasised previously, a conceptual model of the system under study is useful first in order to decide upon the structure of the multiple input–multiple output model.

The first step in the identification stage is to identify, fit and check single output transfer function models for each output separately, using the approach to building such models given in Figure A.6. These single output transfer function models may then be assembled in matrix form as

$$y_t = c + v(B) \otimes \nabla(X_t - \bar{X}) + \psi(B)a_t \tag{A.39}$$

where the matrix $\psi(B)$ is a diagonal matrix. Then, proceeding exactly as for multivariate stochastic models (See Section A.5), the cross and partial cross

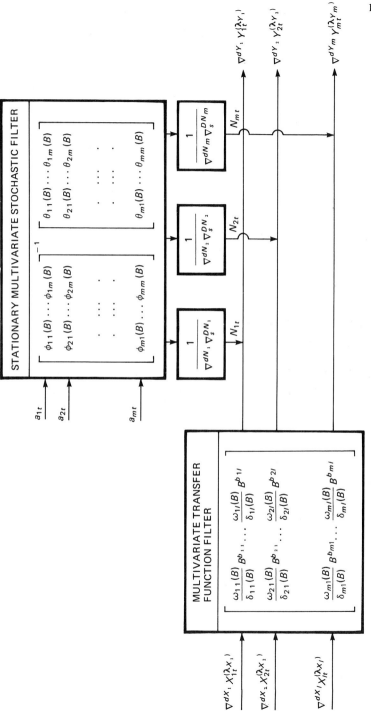

Fig A.10. *Filter representation of seasonal multivariate transfer function—noise model*

correlations of the residual series $\alpha_{it}$ may be used to postulate a multivariate stochastic model

$$\alpha_t = \psi_1(B)a_t \qquad (A.40)$$

for the residuals. Combining (A.39) with (A.40) we obtain an overall model

$$y_t = c + v(B) \otimes \nabla(X_t - \bar{X}) + \psi(B)\psi_1(B)a_t \qquad (A.41)$$

for the appropriately transformed and differenced output series $y_t$ and input series $x_t$. The model (A.41) can now be fitted and checked.

At the checking stage, the following statistics are examined to see whether they reveal model inadequacy:

(i) the residual series $a_{it}$,

(ii) the auto- and cross correlations of the residual series $a_{it}$,

(iii) the cross correlations between each residual series $a_{it}$ and each pre-whitened input $x_{it}$.

At the forecasting stage, the model is realigned if necessary and then forecasts generated, together with the covariance matrix of the forecast errors at each lead time. To generate the forecasts of the outputs, it is necessary to specify:

(a) whether the inputs are to be forecast from a model (for example, a multivariate stochastic model) or whether forecasts external to the model are to be used.

(b) the origins, lead times and probability limits for the forecasts.

An example of building multivariate transfer function models is given in Section 3.5.

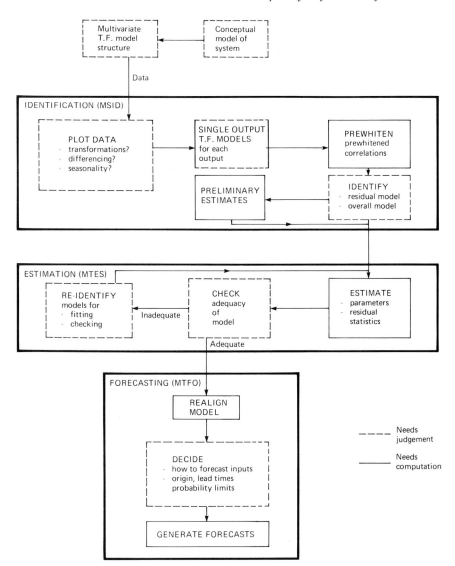

Fig A.11. Flow diagram for multivariate transfer function model building based on three computer programs: MSID (Multivariate Stochastic Identification), MTES (Multivariate Transfer Function Estimation), MTFO (Multivariate Transfer Function Forecasting).

# References

Alavi, A. (1973). Some multivariate extensions of Box–Jenkins forecasting. Ph.D. Thesis, University of Lancaster.

Aström, K. J. (1966). Numerical identification of linear dynamic systems from normal operating records. *Theory of Self-Adaptive Control Systems,* **96** (Plenum Press).

Aström, K. J. (1971). *Introduction to Stochastic Control Theory* (Academic Press, New York).

Bartlett, M. S. (1935). Some aspects of the time-correlation problem in regard to tests of significance. *Jour. Royal Stat. Soc.* **98**, 536.

Bartlett, M. S. and Diananda, P. H. (1950). Extensions of Quenouille's test for autoregressive schemes. *Jour. Royal Stat. Soc.* **B12**, 108.

Bartlett, M. S. and Rajalkashman, D. V. (1953). Goodness-of-fit tests for simultaneous autoregressive series. *Jour. Royal Stat. Soc.* **B15**, 107.

Box, G. E. P., Hillmer, S. C. and Tiao, G. C. (1976). Analysis and modelling of seasonal time-series. N.B.E.R.–Census Conference on seasonal time series, Washington D.C., 1976.

Box, G. E. P. and Jenkins, G. M. (1962). Some statistical aspects of adaptive optimisation and control. *Jour. Royal Stat. Soc.* **B24**, 297.

Box, G. E. P. and Jenkins, G. M. (1963). Further contributions to adaptive quality control: simultaneous estimation of dynamics: non zero costs. *Bull. Intl. Stat. Inst.*, 34th Session, Ottawa, Canada, 943.

Box, G. E. P. and Jenkins, G. M. (1965). Mathematical models for adaptive control and optimisation. *A.I.Ch.E-I.Chem.E.Symp. Series,* **4**, 61.

Box, G. E. P., Jenkins, G. M. and Bacon, D. W. (1967). Models for forecasting seasonal and non-seasonal time series. In: B. Harris, ed., *Advanced Seminar on Spectral Analysis of Time Series*, (John Wiley, New York) 271.

Box, G. E. P. and Jenkins, G. M. (1968). Some recent advances in forecasting and control I. *Applied Stat.* **17**, 91.

Box, G. E. P. and Jenkins, G. M. (1970). *Time Series Analysis, Forecasting and Control* (Holden-Day, San Francisco, 2nd edition, 1976).

Box, G. E. P. and Tiao, G. C. (1975). Intervention analysis with applications to economic and environmental problems. *Jour. Amer. Stat. Assoc.*, **70**, 70.

Box, G. E. P. and Tiao, G. C. (1977). A canonical analysis of multiple time series. *Biometrika,* **64**, 355.

Dhrymes, P. J. (1971). *Distributed Lags: Problems of Formulation and Estimation* (Holden-Day, San Francisco).

Durbin, J. and Watson, G. S. (1950, 1951). Testing for serial correlation in least squares regression, I, II. *Biometrika,* 37, 409; 38, 159.

Durbin, J. (1970). Testing for serial correlation in least-squares regression when some of the regressors are lagged dependent variables. *Econometrica,* 38, 410.

Granger, C. W. J. and Newbold, P. (1976). Identification of two-way causal systems. In: M. D. Intriligator, ed., *Frontiers of Quantitative Economics II* (North-Holland, Amsterdam).

Granger, C. W. J. and Newbold, P. (1977). *Forecasting Economic Time Series* (Academic Press, New York).

Jenkins, G. M. (1975). The interaction between the muskrat and mink cycles in North Canada. *Proceedings of the 8th International Biometric Conference,* Constanta, Roumania, 1974 (Editura Academici Republicii Socialists Românâ, 53, 1975).

Jenkins, G. M. (1977). Review of *"Analysis and Control of Dynamic Economic Systems"* by G. C. Chow. *Jour. Royal Stat. Soc.* A 140, 557.

Jenkins, G. M. and Watts, D. G. (1968). *Spectral Analysis and Its Applications* (Holden-Day, San Francisco).

Jorgensen, D. W. (1966). Rational distributed lag functions, *Econometrica,* 34, 135.

Quenouille, M. H. (1952). *Associated Measurements* (Butterworth, London).

Quenouille, M. H. (1957). *The Analysis of Multiple Time Series* (Charles Griffin, London).

Slutsky, E. (1927). The summation of random causes as the source of cyclical processes. *Problems of Economic Conditions,* 3, No. 1; also in *Econometrica,* 5, 105 (1937).

Tiao, G. C., Box, G. E. P. and Hamming, W. J. (1975). Analysis of Los Angeles photochemical smog data: a statistical overview. *Jour. Air Pollution Control Assoc.,* 25, 260.

Walker, G. (1931). On periodicity in series of related terms. *Proc. Royal Soc.* A 131, 518.

Wilson, G. T. (1973). The estimation of parameters in multivariate time series models. *Jour. Royal Stat. Soc.* B 35, 76.

Yaglom, A. M. (1955). The correlation theory of processes whose $n$'th differences constitute a stationary process. *Matem Sb.,* 37 (79), 141.

Yule, G. U. (1927). On a method of investigating periodicities in disturbed series, with special reference to Wölfer's sunspot numbers. *Phil. Trans.,* A 226, 267.

# Glossary of technical terms

This glossary contains definitions of the technical terms used in the main body of the text. Where possible these definitions have been simplified to make them understandable to non-technical readers. A particular definition may involve terms which are defined elsewhere in the glossary. These cross references are indicated by italics.

**Aligned Models**
**Alignment**

When fitting *multivariate stochastic models* to two or more time series it may be necessary sometimes to shift a series $z_{1t}$ in time by d time units to produce a time series $z_{1,t-d}$ before relating it to another time series $z_{2t}$. The parameter d is called the alignment parameter and the resulting model fitted to the time series $z_{1,t-d}$ and $z_{2t}$ an aligned model.

**Autocorrelation Function**
**Autocorrelation Coefficient**
**Autocorrelated**

A time series in which the current value depends on past values is called an autocorrelated time series. If a series is *stationary* the dependance in the series between two points separated by k time units (the *lag*) can be described by the autocorrelation coefficient $r_k$ at lag k. It measures the extent to which a value of the series above or below the mean at time t tends to be followed by a value of the series above or below the mean k time units later. The plot of $r_k$ against k for k = 1,2, . . . is called the autocorrelation function of the series. It describes how the correlation in the series dies out as the separation or *lag* k between two time points increases. Different models give rise to characteristic autocorrelation patterns. Hence they may be used to recognise which model to fit to a series initially.

## Autoregressive Matrix

A *multivariate stochastic model* may be described in part by an autoregressive matrix which consists of a two dimensional array of *autoregressive operators* $\phi_{ij}$ (B). The operator $\phi_{ij}$ (B) describes how the i'th series is related to past values of the j'th series.

## Autoregressive Models

If a time series has been made *stationary* by *transformation* and *differencing* it may sometimes be possible to represent it by an autoregressive model. In such a model the current value $w_t$ of the *stationary* series is related to p previous values of the series according to

$$(w_t-c) = \phi_1 (w_{t-1}-c) + \ldots + \phi_p(w_{t-p}-c) + a_t$$

where c is the mean of the series and p is called the order of the model. The *random series* $a_t$ is that part of $w_t$ which is unexplained by the model and is called the *residual* — it measures the error in forecasting $w_t$ from a knowledge of $w_{t-1}, \ldots, w_{t-p}$.

## Autoregressive - Moving Average Models

To achieve *parsimony* in parameterisation, that is to represent a *stationary* series by a model involving as few parameters as possible, it may be necessary to build a model containing autoregressive and moving average terms. The resulting model

$$(w_t-c) = \phi_1 (w_{t-1}-c) + \ldots + \phi_p (w_{t-p}-c) + a_t - \theta_1 a_{t-1} - \ldots - \theta_q a_{t-q}$$

is called an autoregressive - moving average model. The current value $w_t$ is related to p previous values $w_{t-1}, \ldots, w_{t-p}$ of the time series and to the current and past values of the residuals or one - step - ahead forecast errors

$a_t, a_{t-1}, \ldots, a_{t-q}$.

## Autoregressive – Integrated Moving Average (ARIMA) Models

A non - seasonal ARIMA Model (see also seasonal ARIMA models) is capable of representing a wide class of *non - stationary* series containing non - deterministic (or stochastic) *trends*. In particular, they are capable of describing series whose level, slope, and if necessary, higher derivatives, are being continuously modified, or adapted, by random shocks entering the system.

Suppose that a *non - stationary* time series is subjected to some form of *data transformation* and *non - seasonal differencing* d times to give a *stationary* time series $w_t$. Then, if no differencing is applied, that is d = 0, an autoregressive - moving average model for $w_t$ enables a wide class of stationary series, in statistical equilibrium about a fixed mean, to be described. However, if the differencing d is greater than zero, the appropriately transformed and differenced series $w_t$ is called an autoregressive - integrated moving average model. In terms of *autoregressive and moving average operators* it can be written

$$\phi(B)\,(\nabla^d z_t\,(\lambda)_- c) \;=\; \theta(B)\,a_t$$

and is referred to as an ARIMA (p, d, q) model where p is the number of *autoregressive parameters,* d is the degree of *non - seasonal differencing* and q is the number of *moving average parameters.*

## Autoregressive Operators
## Autoregressive Parameters

It is convenient sometimes to write an autoregressive model in terms of the *backward shift operator* B such that

$$(1 - \phi_1 B - \ldots - \phi_p B^p)\,(w_t - c) \;=\; a_t$$

where $B^j w_t = w_{t-j}$. The operator

$$\phi(B) = (1 - \phi_1 B - \ldots - \phi_p B^p)$$

is a polynomial of degree p in B and is called an autoregressive operator. This polynomial is very useful in interpreting a model and it is important to know whether its factors are real or imaginary and if imaginary, the size of the period, which corresponds to some cyclical phenomenon in the data. The unknown quantities $\phi_1, \phi_2, \ldots, \phi_p$ which have to be estimated from the observed time series, are called autoregressive parameters.

## Backward Shift Operator

A device for shifting time backwards such that $Bz_t = z_{t-1}$, $B^2 z_t = z_{t-2}$, etc.

## Canonical Analysis
## Canonical Variables

Canonical analysis is a means of simplifying the interpretation of a *multivariate stochastic model*. The canonical variables are linear combinations of the original time series used to build the model possessing simpler correlation properties than the original time series.

## Checking

Procedures to reveal whether there is any evidence of inadequacy in a model fitted to data and, if inadequacy is revealed, the direction in which the model may be elaborated to remove the inadequacy.

## Chi–Squared Statistic

A general statistical procedure for testing the lack of fit of a model. For time series, the chi - squared statistic can be used to test whether a set of *autocorrelations* $r_k$, up to some lag K, of the residuals unexplained by a model reveal any evidence that the residuals are not random. It can also be used to test whether a set of *residual cross correlations* reveal any evidence of inadequacy in a *transfer function model*.

## Correlation Matrix

A two dimensional array of numbers, the element in the i'th row and j'th column measuring the correlation between the i'th parameter and j'th parameter estimates in a model fitted to data. A high positive value of this correlation indicates that a high (low) value of the estimate of the i'th parameter tends to be associated with a high (low) value of the j'th parameter. High positive or negative correlations between parameter estimates are undesirable and reflect ambiguity in the estimation situation since a range of parameter combinations result in models with equally good fits.

## Covariance Matrix of Forecast Errors

Suppose that the *forecast error* of a time series $z_{it}$ from origin t at *lead time* $l$ is $e_{it}(l)$ and that $e_{jt}(l)$ is the corresponding *forecast error* for another time series $z_{jt}$. Then the covariance matrix of the forecast errors at lead time $l$ is a two dimensional array of numbers whose element in the i'th row and j'th column is the covariance between the forecast errors $e_{it}(l)$ and $e_{jt}(l)$. A high covariance indicates that the forecast errors are strongly related.

## Cross Correlation Function
## Cross Correlation Coefficient

If two time series $w_{1t}$ and $w_{2t}$ are *stationary*, the relationship between them can be described in part by the cross correlation coefficient $r_{12}(k)$ which measures the correlation between $w_{1t}$ and $w_{2, t+k}$. The plot of $r_{12}(k)$ against the *lag* k for k = 0, 1, 2, ... is called the cross correlation function. It measures the extent to which a value of the first series above or below the mean tends to be followed by a value of the second series above or below the mean k time units later.

## Data Transformation

Occasionally the *residuals,* or one-step-ahead *forecast errors,* depend on the level of a time series. To make the residuals homogeneous, or independent of the level of the series, it is sometimes necessary to transform the series before building a model, for example by taking logarithms or by raising the data to some suitable power.

## Damped Sine Wave

An undamped sine wave is one which repeats the sine function regularly with a fixed period and amplitude. In a damped sine wave the period remains fixed but the amplitude decays geometrically or exponentially.

## Dummy Variables  (See Intervention Variables)

## Diagnostic Checks  (See Checking)

## Differencing  (See Non-Seasonal Differencing, Seasonal Differencing)

## Dynamic Relationship  (See Lag Structure)

## Error Model
## Error Structure

Any statistical model involves an error or noise which represents that part of the data which can not be explained by the model — it represents the effect of all variables omitted from the model. In non-time series applications it is customary to assume that the errors are *random*. However, in time series models the errors may be *autocorrelated* and hence need to be described by a *univariate stochastic model* which converts the autocorrelated error into a *random* error. Such a model for describing the error is called the error structure or noise structure.

## Estimation

That part of the *model building* process which involves using statistical techniques to determine values (or estimates) of the parameters in a model which has been tentatively postulated at the *identification* stage. The model is said to be fitted to the data.

## Exponentially Weighted Moving Averages

A set of weights applied to the past history of a time series in order to generate a forecast. The weight applied to observation $z_{t-j}$ is $\theta^j (1-\theta)$, that is the weights die out according to an exponential or geometric law. The weights also have the property that their sum is unity, so that the forecast quickly adapts to a change in level of the series. An exponentially weighted moving average forecast is optimal for a model which is such that the first *non-seasonal difference* of the series, or its *transformation,* is a first order *moving average model*

## Forecast

A forecast is characterised by its origin and *lead time.* The origin is the time from which the forecast is made and the lead time is the number of steps ahead that the series is forecast. Thus, the forecast of the future observation $z_{t+l}$ made from origin t at lead time $l$ is denoted by $\hat{z}_t(l)$. A forecast is said to be optimal if it minimises, for each *lead time l*, the mean squared error of the deviations between the observation $z_{t+l}$, when it comes to hand, and its forecast $\hat{z}_t(l)$ from origin t.

## Forecast Error

The forecast error $e_t(l)$ at origin t and *lead time l* is the difference between the observation $z_{t+l}$ when it comes to hand and its forecast $\hat{z}_t(l)$ made at time t.

## Forecast Probability Limits

The future values of a time series can not be forecast with certainty. The uncertainty in a forecast can be described by the probability distribution of the future value $z_{t+l}$ at a lead time $l$ relative to the current origin t. After suitable transformation of the data, this transformed variable can be approximated by a Normal distribution which is characterised by its mean $\mu$ $(l)$ and standard deviation $\sigma(l)$ both of which can be calculated from a knowledge of the model. Thus we can say that the actual observation, when it comes to hand, will have a probability of approximately $a$ of lying between the probability limits

$$\mu(l) \pm u_a \sigma(l)$$

where the values $\pm u_a$ enclose an area $a$ under the Normal distribution with mean zero and standard deviation one.

### Elasticity (See Gain)

### Fitting (See Estimation)

### Gain

A property of *transfer function models.* The full effect of a change in the input (or independent) variable will not affect the output (or dependent) variable immediately. Rather, the effect will build up in time and eventually settle down to a steady state value. The ratio of the eventual change in the output to the change in the input is called the gain or *elasticity* of the model.

### Impulse (or pulse)

A *dummy variable* which takes on a non-zero value at some point in time and is zero elsewhere. It can be used to model the effect of a transient phenomenon such as a strike or a sales promotion.

### Impulse Response Weights

A property of *transfer function models.* The set of weights applied to the past history of an input series in order to calculate an output series.

### Intervention Models

*Transfer function models* in which the input variables are *dummy variables* such as an *impulse* or a *step function.*

### Intervention Variables

*Dummy variables* in the form of *pulses* and *step functions* which can be used to represent mechanisms, such as a temporary change in the level of a time series (for example, due to a strike) or a permanent change in the level of a time series (for example, due to a change in a law), in an intervention model.

## Invertible
## Invertibility

It is reasonable to require that the weights applied to the past history of a time series in order to generate a forecast should die out the further back in time one goes. A model which generates weights with this property is said to be invertible. Otherwise it is said to be non-invertible.

## Lag

The difference k between a time t in a time series and a time $t + k$ in the same or a different time series.

## Lag Structure

The lag structure describes the *dynamic relationship* between an output and an input to a system. An equivalent way of representing such a relationship is by means of a *transfer function*. A general way of representing a linear dynamic relationship or transfer function is by means of a rational lag structure. In this case the transfer function contains an autoregressive component which applies weights to the past values of the output and a moving average component which applies weights to the current and past values of the input, that is

$$Y_t - \delta_1 Y_{t-1} - \dots - \delta_r Y_{t-r} = \omega_0 X_{t-b} - \dots - \omega_s X_{t-b-s}$$

As with other models it is convenient mathematically to write a lag structure in terms of the backward shift operator B as follows:

$$Y_t = \frac{(\omega_0 - \omega_1 B - \dots - \omega_s B^s) B^b X_t}{1 - \delta_1 B - \dots - \delta_r B^r}$$

$$= \frac{\omega(B) B^b X_t}{\delta(B)}$$

where $v(B) = \dfrac{\omega(B) B^b}{\delta(B)}$ is called a transfer function. It is defined by the numbers (r, s, b), where r is the number of autogressive terms, s the number of moving average terms after the first and b the *pure delay*.

**Lead Time**

The number of time intervals ahead that a forecast is made from a given forecast origin.

**Likelihood Functions**
**Likelihood Methods**

Given a *model* involving known values of the parameters, a probability distribution enables one to make statements about possible (unknown) data sets which could be generated by that model. Given the data, their known values can be substituted in the probability distribution, which then becomes a function of the unknown parameters. This function of the parameters is called an inverse probability distribution or a likelihood function. It can be used to rank one's preferences for any combination of values of the parameters. The likelihood function contains all the information in the data about the parameters, given that the model structure is correct. Likelihood methods are concerned with describing the likelihood function in terms of a few numbers. (see maximum likelihood estimates and standard errors).

**Linear Filter**

If the output to a system is obtained by applying a set of weights to past inputs, and adding their contributions, the system is called a linear system or a linear filter. The weights are called the *impulse response weights* of the system.

**Model**

A quantitative model is one which allows a set of dependent (or output) variables to be calculated from a set of independent (or input) variables in numerical form. A quantitative model may take the form of a table of numbers, a graph or set of graphs, or a set of mathematical equations. A conceptual model is one which represents the structure or mechanisms of a model but does not specify the relationships in numerical form.

**Model Adaption**

A device for tuning a model to make it more relevant to a particular time series. Usually the model to be 'tuned' will be a compromise model for a number of time series corresponding to a group of products.

**Model Building**

An iterative process for developing a model starting with a prior information about the problem to hand and with data. It is useful to think of model building as consisting of three steps: *identification* (or specification), *estimation* (or fitting) and *checking* (or criticism). This three step process is repeated iteratively until no evidence is revealed of model inadequacy. Note that a model can never be 'adequate' since, given a sufficiently long length of series, model inadequacies not detectable in a short series, may be revealed.

### Model Monitoring

A device for monitoring the residuals from a model to check whether specific forms of model inadequacy have occurred.

### Moving Average Matrix

A *multivariate stochastic model* may be described in part by a moving average matrix which consists of a two dimensional array of *moving average operators* $\theta_{ij}(B)$. The operator $\theta_{ij}(B)$ describes how the i'th series is related to the past forecast errors of the j'th series.

### Moving Average Models

If a time series has been made *stationary* by *transformation* and *differencing* it may sometimes be possible to represent it by a moving average model. In such a model the current value of the *stationary* series is related to current and previous forecast errors according to

$$w_t - c = a_t - \theta_1 a_{t-1} - \cdots - \theta_q a_{t-q}$$

where c is a constant describing the mean of the series and q is called the order of the model. Whereas the weights applied to past values of the series to generate forecasts from an *autoregressive model* are finite, the weights applied to past values of the series for a *moving average model* are infinite in extent and consist of mixtures of damped exponentials and sine waves.

### Moving Average Operators
### Moving Average Parameters

It is convenient sometimes to write a *moving average model* in terms of the *backward shift operator* B such that

$$w_t - c = (1 - \theta_1 B - \cdots - \theta_q B^q)a_t$$

where $B^j a_t = a_{t-j}$ The operator

$$\theta(B) = (1 - \theta_1 B - \cdots - \theta_q B^q)$$

is called a *moving average operator*. As explained for *autoregressive operators* a knowledge of the real and complex factors of $\theta$ (B) is helpful in interpreting the model and relating it to features in the data. The unknown quantities $\theta_1$, $\theta_2$, ..., $\theta_q$ which have to be estimated from the data are called moving average parameters.

### Multiplicative Models (See Non–Multiplicative Models)

A multiplicative model is one in which, for example for monthly data, the month–to–month behaviour can be separated out from the year–to–year behaviour. From a mathematical point of view it means that the *autoregressive operator*, which dictates the weight to be applied to the past history of the series, can be factorised into a product of a *non–seasonal autoregressive operator* and a number of *seasonal autoregressive operators*, one for each seasonal period. Similarly, the *moving average operator* may be written as the product of *non–seasonal and seasonal moving average operators*.

### Multivariate ARIMA Models (See ARIMA Model)

This model is a generalisation of a *Seasonal ARIMA model* for a single series. It can be used to describe the simultaneous behaviour of several seasonal time series which have mutual dependance or mutual feedback (see Multivariate Stochastic Models).

### Multivariate Stochastic Models

Models which describe the joint behaviour of several time series $z_{1t}$ , ..., $z_{mt}$ which are subject to mutual dependence or mutual feedback, that is changes in one series affect all other series. They contrast with *transfer function models* where the effects are uni–directional, that is changes in the inputs are assumed to affect the outputs but changes in the outputs do not affect the inputs.

### Multivariate Transfer Function Models

Models which contain input variables which affect all outputs uni-directionally (via a transfer function matrix) and noise or error variables which can be described by a *multivariate stochastic model* and which enables all the outputs to affect each other.

### Mutually Uncorrelated Series

A single *random series* is one in which there is no correlation or dependence between the value of the time series at one time point and the value at another time point. A set or vector of mutually uncorrelated series is one in which each series individually is *random* and, in addition, there is no correlation or dependence between the value of one time series at one point and the value of another time series at any time point.

**Noise Model (See Error Model)**

**Noise Structure (See Error Structure)**

**Non - Multiplicative Models (See Multiplicative Models)**

A non-multiplicative model is one in which it is not possible to factorise the *autoregressive and moving average operators* in the form of a product of non-seasonal and seasonal operators.

**Non - Seasonal Autoregressive Operator (See Autoregressive Operator)**

**Non Seasonal Differencing**

The non-seasonal differencing operator $\nabla$ is such that

$$\nabla z_t = z_{t-1}$$

Thus, in the case of monthly data, the value of the series last month is subtracted from this month's value. The non-seasonal differencing operator $\nabla$ may be used to convert a *non-stationary* series $z_t$, containing random jumps in its level, into a stationary series $w_t$. Usually one level of non-seasonal differencing will be adequate to induce stationarity. However, if a series is increasing rapidly, it may be necessary to use second - order differencing, that is

$$\nabla^2 z_t = \nabla \nabla z_t = \nabla(z_t - z_{t-1}) = z_t - 2z_{t-1} + z_{t-2}$$

Second-order differencing enables a *non-stationary* series $z_t$ containing random changes in its level and slope to be converted into a stationary series $w_t$.

**Non - Seasonal Moving Average Operators (See Moving Average Operators)**

**Non - Stationarity**

Whereas a stationary series is one in statistical equilibrium about a fixed mean, a non-stationary series is one whose statistical properties evolve in time. Non-stationary series are characterised by changes in their mean levels, slopes, etc.

## Parsimony

An important property of any model is parsimony which is another example of Occam's razor. A parsimonious model is one which represents the data adequately with the minimum number of parameters. The opposite of parsimony is prodigality. A prodigal model contains too many parameters which will usually be badly estimated since the information in the data is dissipated over too many parameters.

## Partial Autocorrelation Function
## Partial Autocorrelation Coefficient

On the assumption that the model for a *stationary* time series is pure autoregressive, a natural way of determining the order p of the model is to fit *autoregressive models* of orders one, two, three, and so on, to the series. The partial autocorrelation coefficient $s_k$ at lag k is an estimate of the last parameter $\phi_k$ in an *autoregressive model* of order k fitted to the series. It follows that if the order of the *autoregressive model* is p, then all partial autocorrelations for lags k greater than p are zero and hence they may be used to provide initial guesses of the order of the model. The plot of $s_k$ against k is called the partial autocorrelation function.

## Preliminary Estimates

Methods for estimating the parameters in time series models, based on the *likelihood function*, are iterative in nature, the parameters eventually converging to the *maximum likelihood estimates*. To speed up convergence, and to minimise the chance that convergence takes place towards a local maximum in the likelihood function, it is useful to start the estimation process with preliminary guesses of the parameters obtained at the *identification* stage of model building.

## Prewhitening
## Prewhitened Cross Correlation Function

The *cross correlation function* between two *autocorrelated* time series will usually contain spurious values and hence can provide a misleading picture of the relationship between the two time series. In other words, what the cross correlation function is trying to tell us about the relationship between an output $Y_t$ and an input $X_t$ can be obscured by the *autocorrelation function* of either series. To avoid obtaining spurious cross correlations, it is necessary to use the univariate stochastic model for the input series to convert it into random series $a_t$, that is to prewhiten the input. The same model applied to the output series will convert it to a series $\beta_t$ which, in general, will not be random. The prewhitened cross correlation function is the *cross correlation function* between the prewhitened input $a_{t-k}$ and the correspondingly filtered output $\beta_t$ at lags k = 0, 1, 2 . . . It can be used to identify a relationship between $Y_t$ and $X_t$.

### Pure Delay

A change in an input series to a *transfer function model* may not begin to affect an output series for b time intervals. The parameter b is called the pure delay of the *transfer function model.* It will need to be estimated from the data, along with other parameters in the model.

### Random Series

A random series is the simplest possible structure for a time series. Its *autocorrelations* are zero at all *lags.* The best forecast of a random series is its mean since a future value is just as likely to lie above as below the mean. The objective in time series analysis is to fit a model to the series so that what is left unexplained by the model is a random series.

### Random Walk

A random walk $z_t$ is the sum of a random series $a_t$ up to time t, that is

$$z_t = a_t + a_{t-1} + a_{t-2} + \cdots$$

Alternatively, a random walk is such that, after *non-seasonal differencing,* the series is *random*, that is

$$\nabla z_t = z_t - z_{t-1} = a_t$$

If $z_t$ is the distance travelled at time t by a walker walking along a straight line, $\nabla z_t$ is the length of the step taken by the walker from time t−1 to time t. Hence the walker takes random steps (which implies that he is probably drunk!). If the mean of the random series $a_t$ is zero, the expected value of the sum $z_t$ is also zero. However, at any point in time, the sum of the series is most unlikely to be zero. In fact, a random walk can drift in one direction for a considerable period of time.

### Range - Mean Plot

The range of a series of observations is the difference between the largest and smallest value. The mean of these same observations is the sum (taking into account the sign) of the observations divided by the number of observations. A rough indication of the *data transformation* needed to generate homogeneous residuals from a time series model can be obtained by dividing the time series into sub-series and calculating the range and mean of each sub-series. The plot of the range of a sub-series against its mean is called a range-mean plot. The pattern, if any, in a range-mean plot can be used to guess the *transformation* to be applied to the time series (See Appendix A1).

## Rational Lag Structures  (See Lag Structures)

## Regression Models
## Regression Analysis

Given observations on a dependent (or output) variable $Y_t$ and independent (or input) variables $X_{1t}, X_{2t}, \ldots, X_{lt}$, a linear regression model is one in which the output is related to the input by a relationship of the form

$$Y_t = b_0 + b_1 X_{1t} + \ldots + b_l X_{lt} + a_t$$

where $b_0, b_1, \ldots, b_l$ are unknown parameters, called regression coefficients, to be estimated from the data, and $a_t$ is a *random series* with mean zero and variance $\sigma_a^2$. Regression analysis was designed for analysing data not in the form of time series. Its application to the analysis of time series is fraught with dangers since the regression coefficients can be spurious (see *prewhitening*) and the *residuals* $a_t$ may be highly *autocorrelated*. These difficulties can be avoided in building *transfer function models*, of which regression models are a very special case.

## Residuals

The part of the data which cannot be explained by a statistical model. In time series analysis, as in all other areas of statistics, the objective is to convert the data into a series of residuals which are *random* with zero mean and a constant variance. When analysing multivariate time series there will be a set of residuals associated with each output time series. Each residual series must be random and *mutually uncorrelated* with any other residual series except possibly at simultaneous times. The properties of residuals mentioned above are important and form the basis of the *checking* (criticism) stage of model building.

## Residual Autocorrelations
## Residual Autocorrelation Function

The residual autocorrelation function consists of the plot of the residual autocorrelations $r_a(k)$ against the *lag* k. Theoretically, the residual autocorrelation function of a series of *random* residuals should be zero for all lags. In practice, they will display fluctuations due to the finite length of the time series. One check for model inadequacy is that the residual autocorrelations are large compared with their *standard errors,* calculated under the assumption that the series is *random.*

## Residual Cross Correlations
## Residual Cross Correlation Function

For a transfer function model to contain no evidence of inadequacy, it is not sufficient for the *residuals* to be random. An important further check is that the residuals are uncorrelated at all *lags* with each input series. This is because any inadequacy in the transfer function will 'leak' into the noise and the residuals — which are then bound to be cross correlated with the input series. To check whether this leakage is happening, the residuals must be cross correlated with the prewhitened input series (if no *prewhitening* is carried out, the cross correlations could be spurious due to the presence of *autocorrelation* in the input). If the prewhitened series is $a_t$ and the residual series $a_t$, the residual cross correlation function is denoted by $r_{aa}(k)$ and is the plot of the cross correlation between $a_t$ and $a_{t+k}$ for each lag $k = 0, 1, 2, \ldots$

## Residual Variance
## Residual Standard Deviation

The *residuals* $a_t$ from a model represent that part of the data which can not be explained by the model. The measure which is normally used to characterise the average 'size' of the residuals is their variance. Since the fitting process ensures that the mean of the residuals is zero, the variance is estimated by the mean of the squares of the residuals. Hence, the units of the residual variance are the square of the units of the original series (or its transform if the data is transformed). The residual *standard deviation,* which is the square root of the residual variance, is a more relevant quantity for measuring the 'size' of the residuals and for comparing alternative models. For *univariate stochastic models* the residual standard deviation is also the standard deviation of the one-step-ahead forecasts generated by the model. Hence, the probability limits for the one-step-ahead forecasts (and also for forecasts several steps ahead) will be directly proportional to the residual standard deviation.

## Seasonality
## Seasonal Period

If it is known that a time series contains a component due to a regular cycle with a fixed period, the series is said to exhibit seasonality. It is important that the cycle is determined from factors which are external to the data rather than by inspection of the data itself. Sometimes the data will contain cyclic behaviour with random changes in amplitude, phase and period, such as a business cycle. Such quasi-cyclical phenomena are best described by *autoregressive models* and should not be treated as seasonal phenomena. Examples of seasonality are monthly sales of ice cream or heating oil (period = 12), hourly energy consumption (period = 24) and daily traffic flow (periods = 7 and 365).

## Seasonal Adjustment
## Seasonal Component

It is conventional in economics to decompose a time series into a 'trend', 'seasonal component' and 'random component'. To enable the direction of the 'trend' at a given instant to be seen more clearly, methods exist for removing the 'seasonal component'. Such techniques are called seasonal adjustment methods (See Section 4.1)

## Seasonal ARIMA Model

A seasonal ARIMA model is a generalisation of a *non-seasonal ARIMA model*. It is capable of describing a wide range of practical time series containing random changes in level, slope etc. and random changes in level, slope etc. of their seasonal patterns.

Suppose that a non-stationary series is subjected to some form of *data transformation, non-seasonal differencing* of order d and *seasonal* differencing of order D in order to convert it into a stationary time series $w_t$. Then a seasonal ARIMA model may be written in operator notation as

$$\phi(B)\Phi(B^S)(w_t - c) = \theta(B)\,\Theta\,(B^S)a_t$$

where the *autoregressive and moving average operators* are defined elsewhere in the glossary. A seasonal ARIMA model may be thought of as describing two effects simultaneously. For example, if the data is monthly, the month-to-month behaviour is assumed to be described by a non-seasonal ARIMA model with parameters (p, d, q). Then the residuals from this model are assumed to be represented by a year-to-year ARIMA model with parameters (P, D, Q). On combining these two models we obtain the above seasonal ARIMA (p, d, q) × $(P, D, Q)_S$ model.

## Seasonal Autoregressive Operator

A seasonal autoregressive operator is an *autoregressive operator* which picks out every s'th value of the series, where s is the seasonal period, that is

$$\Phi(B^S)w_t = (1 - \Phi_1 B^S - \ldots - \Phi_p B^{Ps})w_t$$

$$= w_t - \Phi_1 w_{t-s} - \ldots - \Phi_p w_{t-Ps}$$

The factors of the seasonal autoregressive operator are helpful in interpreting the seasonal part of a model in the same way that the factors of a non-seasonal autoregressive operator are helpful in interpreting the non-seasonal part of a model.

### Seasonal Differencing

The seasonal differencing operator $\nabla_s$ with period s is such that

$$\nabla_s z_t = z_t - z_{t-s}$$

Thus, for monthly data, the value of the series in a given month has subtracted from it the value of the series in the same month in the previous year and hence $\nabla_s$ measures the annual change in level. The seasonal differencing operator may be used to convert a series which is *non-stationary* with respect to its seasonal component into a stationary series. As with *non-seasonal differencing,* it may sometimes be necessary to use second-order seasonal differencing to induce stationarity in the seasonal component, that is

$$\nabla_s^2 z_t = \nabla_s \nabla_s z_t = \nabla_s(z_t - z_{t-s}) = z_t - 2z_{t-s} + z_{t-2s}$$

### Seasonal Moving Average Operator

A seasonal moving average operator is a *moving average operator* which picks out every s'th value of the *residual* series $a_t$, where s is the *seasonal period,* that is

$$\Theta(B^S)a_t = (1 - \Theta_1 B^S - \ldots - \Theta_Q B^{Qs})a_t$$

$$= a_t - \Theta_1 a_{t-s} - \ldots - \Theta_Q a_{t-Qs}$$

Like *seasonal autoregressive operators,* seasonal moving average operators may be factorised in order to generate insight into the seasonal part of a model.

### Standard Deviation
### Standard Error

The standard deviation is a measure of the spread or scatter of a probability distribution about its mean. It can be used to calculate *probability limits* between which an observation selected at random will lie with a specified probability level $a$.

A standard error is a measure of the spread (or scatter) of the probability distribution of the estimate of a model parameter obtained from a finite length of series. It can be used to calculate limits of accuracy, called confidence intervals, for the parameter. Alternatively, the standard error can be thought of as measuring the spread (or the inverse curvature) of the likelihood function, a high spread corresponding to a high standard error and a low spread corresponding to a small standard error.

## Step Function

A *dummy variable* which is zero up to a certain point and takes on the value one, or some other constant, thereafter. It can be used to model a permanent change in the level or slope of a time series.

## Stationary Time Series
## Stationarity

A time series which is in a state of statistical equilibrium, that is its statistical properties do not evolve in time, is called a stationary time series. In particular, a stationary time series has a constant mean, constant variance and the correlation between observations at times t and t+k is the same as the correlation between observations at times $t+t_1$ and $t+t_1+k$. These correlations are called *autocorrelations*.

## Transformation  (See Data Transformation)

## Transfer Function Models  (See Multivariate Transfer Function Models)

A single output transfer function model relates an output variable $Y_t$ to several related input series $X_{1t}, X_{2t}, \ldots, X_{lt}$, it being assumed that the inputs affect the output but that the output does not affect the inputs. To the extent that the inputs do not fully explain the output it is necessary to add a *noise model* or *error model* which describes the discrepancies. In general, a transfer function-noise model may be written

$$Y_t = v_1(B)X_{1t} + \ldots + v_l(B)X_{lt} + N_t$$

where $v_i(B)$ is a transfer function with *rational lag structure* applied to the i'th variable and $N_t$ is a noise model which is a *seasonal ARIMA model*.

A transfer function model determines what weight should be applied to the past history of the output series and the current and past values of the inputs in order to forecast future values of the input series.

## Trend

It is customary to call a change in the level of a *non-stationary* time series a trend. It has also been customary to represent such trends by mathematical functions of time, such as polynomials, which imply that the trend is deterministic. However, many trends which occur in practice are non-deterministic (or stochastic) that is the way in which the series evolves is influenced by random shocks. Such non-deterministic trends are better represented by non-stationary models involving *non-seasonal differencing* and *seasonal differencing*. (See Section 4.2)

## Univariate Stochastic Models

A univariate stochastic model attempts to forecast a time series $z_t$ from its past history only. Thus the forecast can be written as

$$\text{Forecast} = \pi_1 z_t + \pi_2 z_{t-1} + \pi_3 z_{t-2} + \ldots$$

Different univariate stochastic models correspond to different choices of the weights $\pi_j$ applied to past observations. To achieve *parsimony* a model must be developed so that the weights $\pi_j$ can be expressed in terms of as few parameters as possible, as in a *seasonal ARIMA model.*